D1358860

Father to Nobody's Children

The Life
of
Thomas J. Barnardo

Father to Nobody's Children

David E. Fessenden

CLC ❖ PUBLICATIONS
Fort Washington, Pennsylvania 19034

Published by CLC ❖ Publications

U.S.A.
P.O. Box 1449, Fort Washington, PA 19034

GREAT BRITAIN
51 The Dean, Alresford, Hants. SO24 9BJ

AUSTRALIA
P.O. Box 419M, Manunda, QLD 4879

NEW ZEALAND
10 MacArthur Street, Feilding

ISBN 0-87508-662-4

Copyright © 1995
David E. Fessenden

This printing 2005

Contents

1

∞

"Sir, May I Stay?"

THE young man was just ending a full day. Following his studies at medical school, he had conducted evening classes in reading, writing, arithmetic and Bible for poor boys in the slums of London. Now the last class of the evening was over, all the young scholars had gone, and he began to close up shop, not at all aware that he was about to have an encounter that would change his life.

His name was Thomas J. Barnardo, and he was studying to become a medical missionary to China. When he wasn't hitting the books, he could be found preaching in the street or teaching in a small "ragged school" (so called because of the condition of the clothes of the poor boys who attended there).

This particular night, he was closing up the school he and his friends had started in an old donkey shed. It wasn't as bad as it sounds; after they had laid down some wooden planks over the dirt floor and whitewashed the walls, it was not too bad. It was certainly no worse than many of the homes these boys lived in here in the East End of London.

It was time to put out the fire in the hearth. But as he turned toward the fireplace he noticed a little figure standing there, staring into the flames. Not all the scholars were gone after all! But this boy could hardly be called a scholar; the young medical student recognized him as the quiet little lad who had sneaked in late and paid little attention to the lesson. He had probably come in just to get out of the cold.

"Come, my lad, it's time to go home now," said Barnardo. "You're lucky I noticed you; I almost closed up the school for the night and left you locked in here!"

"That would suit me just fine, sir!" the child said eagerly.

"Whatever do you mean? If you were locked in here all night, your mother would be worried sick about you."

"I ain't got no mother, sir."

"No mother? Well, your father, then. Now run along home."

"I ain't got no father, sir. And I ain't got no home to go to."

By now the young man was growing impatient. "Enough of this, now! Get along to your friends or wherever you live."

"I ain't got no friends, sir. And I told you—I don't

live nowhere!" The boy stuck a defiant, dirty chin up in the air.

Now the young medical student was even more puzzled. Was this boy pulling his leg? Could there really be a child in this modern year of 1866 with no place to stay?

"Come over here, lad," Barnardo said gently, and as the child shuffled over to him weakly, any doubts he had as to the truth of the story faded away. The boy was dressed in rags that could hardly have kept him warm on such a cold night. He was frighteningly thin, and covered with dirt. Barnardo had worked for a while in the slums, and he thought he had seen poverty; but this child was without shirt, shoes or socks—in the middle of the winter!

"How old are you, son?" Barnardo said, after a long time.

"Ten, sir," he replied. He was small for his age, but his face looked older; his eyes had the hard, tired look of a suffering old man. His sad face and the painful tone in his voice had a ring of truth in them.

"Do you mean to tell me, child," Barnardo asked again, "that you have no home, no father or mother or friends?"

"That's right sir. I'm not lying."

"Then where did you sleep last night?"

"In a hay wagon, down at the market. Then today I met another boy, who told me I could come here to get warm. He said you might let me stay by the fire all night. Oh, please, sir! May I stay? I won't do no harm."

It was a cold winter night, with a raw wind that seemed to blow right through you; and a horrible thought sprang to Barnardo's mind: *Is it possible that there are other children in the city of London like this boy—cold, hungry, homeless?*

The boy was awaiting his decision. "Tell me, lad," he said hesitantly, "are there other poor boys like you in London, without a home or family?"

The boy smiled grimly, and looked at Barnardo the way a child does when an adult asks a stupid question. "Of course, sir; heaps of 'em! More 'n I could count!"

This was too much for Barnardo; surely the boy was lying! But then he had an idea! "My lad," he said, "if I were to give you something to eat and a place to sleep, would you take me to where some of these homeless boys sleep? Could you show me their hiding places?"

The child's eyes lit up like a hungry wolf, and he eagerly nodded his head.

As the pair walked to the medical student's apartment, around the corner from the London Hospital, the child was quiet as a mouse; all Barnardo heard out of him was the soft padding of his bare feet on the pavement. He walked along with his ragged clothes wrapped tightly around him, in a vain attempt to keep out the biting wind. Once again, Barnardo thought back on the boy's incredible story. Homeless boys, sleeping outside in the dead of winter? More than he could count? Impossible! Yet in the back of his mind an insistent voice kept asking, *Suppose, after all, he speaks the truth?*

Upon reaching his home, Barnardo wasted no time. He placed the boy at his table and quickly supplied him with food and a hot drink. It was amazing how quickly he ate—at least that part of his story was no lie! And the meal did wonders for him; in a decidedly stronger voice, he told his story.

"My name's Jim," he said between mouthfuls. "Jim Jarvis. Never knew my father, and Mother was always sick. When I was just a little kid, she went into the hospital and I was sent to a poor boys' school. After Mother died I runned away."

"How long ago was that?"

"Don't exactly know, sir—but it was more than five years ago."

"Where did you go then?"

"There was an old lady down near Wapping that knowed my mother. She let me sleep in a shed out back. She was very kind to me. After that, I did odd jobs on a barge for a man they called Swearin' Dick. He treated me very bad, sir; he used to knock me around when I hadn't done nothin' and sometimes he wouldn't give me anything to eat. Sometimes he'd go away for days and leave me by myself on the boat."

"Well," Barnardo asked, "why didn't you run away?"

"I thought about it many a time," Jim replied, and some of his sad expression returned to his now-happy face. "But Dick swore he'd kill me if I did. He had a big, mean dog and he made it smell me—and he told me that if I ever tried to leave the barge, he'd send the dog after me. Sometimes when he was drunk, he'd sic the dog on me just for fun. Look here, sir, at what he did to me once."

And he pulled aside his rags to reveal a long scar that ran down his leg.

"How did you get away?" Barnardo asked.

"Well, one day when Dick was away, a man stopped by the boat and said Dick wasn't coming back—he joined the army when he was drunk. So I said, 'Mister, can you hold that dog for a minute?' And when he went down the hatchway with the dog, I shut the hatch on 'em both and runned away as fast as I could!"

In spite of himself, the medical student couldn't hold back a smile at the thought of Jim's quick-thinking escape!

Jim Jarvis told how he had been doing well, getting some odd jobs and begging a penny now and then. "But since the cold came on, I ain't had no luck at all. I've been sleepin' out hungry 'most every night."

"Well, Jim, if you're willing, I could find you a home where you could have plenty to eat and drink, good friends to take care of you, and even a chance to go to school."

"That'd suit me just fine, sir!"

"Then we'll see about that tomorrow. But first, there is one more thing I want to ask you: have you ever heard of another world where there is no hunger and cold, where children will never be beaten or treated badly?"

"You mean heaven, sir?"

"That's right, heaven," Barnardo smiled. "It's a wonderful place—but to go there you must know Jesus. Do you know Him, Jim?"

"Yes," he said eagerly. "I know who He is. He's the Pope!"

Barnardo looked at him with astonishment. "Who told you that, Jim?"

"No one, sir; but I knows I'm right," he said with a nod, "because when my mother used to talk about the Pope, she'd do this"—and he made the sign of the cross across his chest—"and later, when she was dyin', a man in black came and talked to her about Jesus, and they both did the same."

"So when your mother made the same sign with her fingers when she spoke about Jesus and the Pope, you figured they were the same person, eh?"

"That's it, sir!" and he smiled, quite pleased with himself.

"Jim, I'm afraid you are mistaken," Barnardo said. "Let me tell you the real story of Jesus." And he proceeded to explain how Christ came to earth as a baby in Bethlehem, of His goodness and kindness toward everyone, of His love for children. Jim was fascinated; this was all new to him. Throughout the story, he asked many questions which the medical student tried his best to answer. Because of Jim's limited education and experience, Barnardo had to explain some of the simplest details. But it was evident that poor Jim understood, and when he heard about Christ's death on the cross, he broke down in tears.

"Oh, sir!" he cried. "That's worse than anything Swearin' Dick ever did to me!" It was obvious that through Barnardo's simple words, little Jim had grown to love this Jesus—and now He was dead!

"But wait, Jim. The story doesn't end there," Barnardo added, and he told how Christ rose from the dead and lives forever in heaven. Then he knelt and prayed that the Lord would bless young Jim.

It was after midnight when the pair set off in search of the homeless boys. This time Jim confidently held Barnardo's hand. After crossing several main streets, Jim led his companion through a maze of back alleys. They passed small, dingy storefronts—locked, shuttered, and silent.

Finally they came to a shabby old shed where used clothing was sold. This was a bustling place of business in the daytime, but tonight everything was empty and still. They entered the shed and began a search, but it was soon obvious that it was deserted.

"Never mind, sir; they aren't here," Jim said at last, and for a moment Barnardo thought he might confess that it was all a hoax. "They don't dare lay about here, or the police would catch 'em. Once, when I was green, I slept around here, but I nearly got nabbed, so I don't do that no more."

He led Barnardo through the shed and back into the alley, which ended at a brick wall—the side of a building.

Jim put his finger to his lips. "Shh! In a minute we'll see lots of 'em, sir, if we don't wake 'em up."

"But Jim," Barnardo whispered, "*where* are they?"

"Up there," Jim replied, and before Barnardo could ask what he meant, Jim scrambled up the side of the wall like a monkey. Then he held down a stick for Barnardo to grasp, and the medical student managed, after some time, to hoist himself up so he could peer over the edge of the rooftop.

Spread out on the flat roof lay eleven boys, some curled up by themselves, others huddled together for warmth. They had nothing to cover them, and their clothes were, if possible, in even worse condition than Jim's. One was older, probably about eighteen; the rest varied in age from maybe nine to fourteen.

At that moment, the full moon came out from behind a cloud, shining on the faces of the sleeping boys. To Barnardo, it was as if God had pulled aside a curtain and showed him a dreadful secret. These poor children were absolutely homeless and destitute—and surely they were just a handful of many others who were cold and alone, with no place to live.

Barnardo had worked for a while among the poor in London, and he knew of many children who lived in tiny, dingy rooms and had little to eat. But the depth of poverty that he saw that night was totally unknown to him, and even now he almost doubted what he beheld with his own eyes.

"Shall I wake 'em, sir?"

Barnardo had been lost in thought, and Jim's question startled him. He looked on the child's face and saw no trace of the shock and pain that he himself felt; scenes such as this were commonplace for the boy.

"No, don't wake them," Barnardo replied after a moment. He had already decided to do what he could to help Jim, but he knew he couldn't care for eleven others. Instead, he breathed a silent prayer for them and began the awkward climb down to the street.

Jim was down to his side in a moment. "Would you like me to show you another sleeping place, sir? There's lots more!"

"No, I've seen enough," Barnardo said. Deep inside, he could hear the Lord speaking to him: *You must help these boys.* He wanted to say, "Yes, Lord," but what could he do? He was just a medical student, with no experience in these things and no money to help. But there and then he did resolve to help, and to trust God to show him how.

From that single decision grew a ministry that helped tens of thousands of homeless children, brought many to faith in Christ, and even changed the laws of the British government. But who was this Thomas Barnardo, and what led him to the slums of London in the first place?

2

✣

A Man Called by God

THOMAS JOHN BARNARDO was born in Dublin, Ireland, in 1845. He came from Spanish stock, as his name suggests, but the family left their native land because of religious persecution—they were one of the few Protestant families in the country which had given the world the Inquisition. The Barnardo clan settled in Germany, but Thomas' father later moved to Ireland and became a British citizen.

Thomas was very sickly at birth and continued to be in poor health in his early childhood. One day at the age of two he lost consciousness and appeared to have died. The grieving family handed the tiny body over to the undertaker, but as he began to prepare the body for burial he noted a faint movement. Soon the family had their little boy back, as if from the dead.

His mother was of Quaker background and had a strong influence on her children. He attended Sunday school at the local Anglican church, and was confirmed by the Archbishop of Dublin at about fifteen. By his own admission, he did not know the Lord as his Savior at that time.

At the age of ten he was sent to school. There he encountered what was probably his first experience of truly ill treatment, under a principal who was a clergyman, no less. "He seemed to take a savage delight in beating his boys," Barnardo recalled thirty-five years later with vivid clarity. "There were two or three unfortunate lads in the school who were the special subjects of his unceasing persecution." The young boy never forgot those years of harsh treatment. When later he taught school himself, he probably leaned a bit too much in the opposite extreme, being a bit too easy-going when a firmer hand was needed.

His brother described him as "full of fun and mischief, thoughtless and careless." Though he loved and respected his parents, he was a handful, and gave them some trouble. Possibly because of his early illnesses, he was not that interested in sports. His main pleasure was in reading; he read voraciously, and not always with discernment. As a result, he dabbled in the works of such unbelieving men as Voltaire and Rousseau. At the age of fourteen he announced that he was an atheist, much to the pain of his mother.

It was at this time that a revival began in parts of

Ireland. Thomas' mother and two brothers had come to faith in Christ through this movement. They regularly took Thomas with them to the services in a Dublin meeting place known as Metropolitan Hall. He attended very reluctantly and did not appear to be influenced much by the preaching.

"After the meetings we always remained, and then some Christians would come up to me and ask me if I had found Jesus," he wrote in a letter to his sister in 1862. "I used to think the people were mad." Still captivated by the arguments of the skeptics, he often scoffed at the events at these meetings. "I know I behaved very badly," he commented on his actions at one home meeting. "I was just as cheeky as a young fellow can be." However, one evening he attended a home meeting where John Hambleton, the converted actor, spoke. The wind was blown out of the young skeptic's sails, and he was very quiet on the way home. Later that night he went into the room of one of his brothers in a very disturbed state of mind. He confessed how the words of Hambleton had touched him deeply and he could not get to sleep. Soon the three brothers were kneeling on the floor, crying and praying as Thomas entered the kingdom of God.

His new-found faith was immediately translated into fervent evangelism as he began working with a "ragged school" in a poor section of Dublin. An early pupil of these classes remembered a time when young Barnardo spoke with such earnestness that one lad was converted right on the spot.

He also visited the sick, soldiers in their barracks, and the officers at the local police station, sharing his testimony. He quickly took an interest in the poor and would often stop at a local home for widows with packets of tea for the ladies.

In only a few months, he felt he was ready to do more. His admiration for the faith and ministry of George Mueller led him to contact the preacher in Bristol for advice. After referring to the conversion of "seven members of my own family and myself within the last five months," he told how he had the idea of renting a hall and holding revival prayer meetings with some friends of his. "I have been bringing the matter for some time back before the Lord, and today after rising from my knees the finger of the Lord appeared to point me to you and to abide by your advice." Mueller replied that perhaps the young man, at the age of seventeen and only a few months old in the Lord, might better spend his time studying the Word.

Despite the advice, he and his brothers did rent some rooms and held evangelistic meetings once or twice a week. He also began work in a rough section of town known as The Liberties; it was hard ground to plow and many people opposed him, but some good was done and he probably learned a little about urban ministry—experience that would help him later in life.

Soon he decided to prepare for full-time Christian work, and joined a Bible-and-theology class being conducted in a private home. At one of those meetings the teacher arranged for Hudson Taylor, founder of the China Inland Mission, to speak to the students. Mr. Taylor was very well-known even back then, and the young men were greatly anticipating his message. As they waited in a room for the message to begin, the teacher stepped in, apparently alone.

"Where is the great man?" Barnardo whispered to a companion.

Then the teacher stepped aside and a short, unassuming man took the podium. Thomas, who had always been self-conscious about his height, whispered again to his companion, "Why, there is hope for me yet!" After the meeting, young Barnardo stayed behind to talk to the missionary, and afterward was convinced that he was called to go to China. He even wrote a poem about it that he had published. Within three months he was in London to prepare for missionary service.

As Mr. Taylor observed this young candidate, he

sensed that the Lord had other work for him and suggested a career as a medical missionary. So it was that Thomas arrived in London in April of 1866, saw his friends off on a ship bound for China in May, then began his studies at London Hospital—all alone in a city he hardly knew. For some young men, being alone and away from parental influence could have been a temptation; for Barnardo it was an opportunity for ministry.

Just opposite the hospital was Mile End Waste, a wide-open space where people gathered to listen to and debate the topics of the day. Like the Apostle Paul in Athens, Barnardo saw a chance to say a word for the Lord. He would often stop there after a long day of study and work, and join in the discussion. His early reading of Voltaire and Rousseau proved to be useful in these debates; he knew the arguments of unbelievers and had long ago found the biblical answer to them. Occasionally he would even preach to the crowds.

Barnardo was already a bit of an oddball to the other medical students, since he was a bit older (or at least he acted older) than most of them. He was known for being courteous, friendly and enthusiastic, but he just didn't act the same. It was obvious that he was involved in other activities outside the college and hospital, and this caused the other medical students to wonder what he was up to. A fellow student who later became an eminent physician described the conversation between the students about Barnardo as going something like this:

"Queer fellow, Barnardo."

"Yes, what's wrong with that man?"

"Seems to me he's got something on his mind."

"He's up to something. I wonder what his little game is?"

"He has brains, you know; I shouldn't wonder if he's doing a little extra studying on the sly."

"No, he can't be. He missed a question the professor asked the other day."

"Does he bet? Is he seeing a woman?"

"Doesn't look like it."

"You know, someone saw him preaching in the street the other day."

At this, the whole group exclaimed, "Preaching?"

"Good heavens! A religious crackpot!"

"The hypocrite—no wonder we don't like him!"

"He'll be starting a prayer meeting here next."

"It's a disgrace to the hospital; let's stay away from him."

Being rejected by most of the other medical students didn't seem to bother him greatly. He did have a few college friends, and he had so little in common with the others that it didn't really matter. So many of them were concerned only with the physical body and how to advance their medical career. Barnardo's interest in the soul and eternal rewards was completely foreign to them.

One fellow student encountered him preaching on the street one day and was amazed at his speaking skill: "His ability and sincerity were appreciated by the people, who were silent and remained to the end of the address. I have been informed by those who heard him most often that in supporting his views he always rather more than held his own. It certainly seemed so to me. On his return from one of these occasions, his face generally wore its happiest expression—not that, I thought, of triumph, but of the joy of battle that remains with the strong and resourceful."

Not all his preaching was so successful. One time he spoke to a crowd and concluded it with prayer. As he stood with his head bowed and his eyes closed, a young rascal on the edge of the crowd was busy making a hard ball of mud with some gutter water and street sweepings. The boy took a good windup and shot the mud ball right at the young preacher. "I had just opened my mouth in prayer," Barnardo later recalled, "when lo and behold, it was neatly and tightly plugged. . . . I could neither shut my mouth nor eject the missile! Of course I instantly opened my eyes and found everyone around me convulsed with laughter! The boy was gone."

Barnardo had a natural interest in children and experience with ragged schools in Dublin. That is probably what led him to work with a school in his London neighborhood—Ernest Street Ragged School. He displayed an uncanny ability to keep order among the unruly boys that made up his class. After a few months, the committee that ran the institution made him superintendent.

Once when he admired a friend's walking stick, the fellow asked Barnardo if he ever used one. Barnardo replied that he used to carry one, but found that when the boys in his class annoyed him it was too tempting to use it as a vent for his anger. "If I had, it would have killed my work for the Lord, so I left it home after that."

During all this time, he was still studying at the hospital, where he increasingly became a loner. Few of his fellow students knew the full extent of his work in the East End, and fewer still appreciated it. Their feelings changed greatly as the years went by and the importance of Barnardo's ministry came to light. But in his student days, while he was still unknown, most of the other medical students ignored him or even made fun of him.

But his ragged-school students loved him. And

he loved them, and was especially upset to see so many of them leading lives that were sure to take them down the wrong road. The influences on these children were horrible. One common pastime of many of the boys and girls in his school was the "penny gaff," a cheap theater amusement offered for the cost of a penny. This exposed the children to "adult" entertainment that was inappropriate for their age. The young medical student decided one day to look the problem over firsthand. He entered one of the theaters and observed with great concern the things taking place on stage. He then looked over the crowd, some of whom he recognized as his own students. "I looked down from a side box [balcony seat] upon their eager faces, drinking in the abominations of the place," he later wrote.

The situation could not go on, he decided. Upon finding the owner of the place, he asked for permission to speak to the young people between acts. The owner agreed—provided he pay for the privilege. Though the price he asked was outrageous, Barnardo paid it, feeling the opportunity could not be passed up.

So the rowdy crowd was astonished when the curtain rose to reveal, not the villain of the play they had been watching, but their schoolteacher! This was a real sight and many cheers and much laughter went up from the audience. It took some time for Barnardo to quiet them down, and he could only do so by promising to sing a song. Upon finishing his solo, he began to preach about the harmful influence they were letting themselves be exposed to and vividly described the joys of the Christian life.

The owner soon realized this was going to ruin his business, so he rushed up on the stage and demanded that Barnardo stop preaching. "Well, I will leave if you insist upon it," Barnardo replied, "but in that case, as you have broken your bargain, you must give me back my money and allow me to tell the boys why I leave." The owner grudgingly gave him a partial refund as Barnardo said, "My lads, I am not allowed to finish what I had to say to you, but if you care to listen I shall be outside." Then he disappeared behind the curtain amid the cheers of the crowd.

In seconds the theater was empty. The entire audience left to go out and hear the schoolteacher. Barnardo found a wooden box to stand on and spoke the gospel to them in plain and simple words. Finally he ended with a short prayer for the young boys. The crowd broke up as the children cried out, "G'night, sir!" "Thank you!" and "God bless you!"

Another one of his attempts at invading Satan's territory didn't end so happily.

3

⧂⧃

Thrust Into the Limelight

IN ADDITION to teaching, Barnardo used literature to spread the gospel. In fact, he came to be known around the neighborhood as the little man with a parcel under his arm; he was always carrying a collection of gospel tracts to give to anyone who would take them.

Barnardo used to buy quantities of Bibles and New Testaments to sell at a reasonable price. One day he boldly entered a barroom and offered his books for sale to all those present. After making sales to those in the front room, he decided to try the back room. The bartender tried to discourage him, saying he could not be responsible for any violence. But Barnardo had prayed for guidance before he set out that day, as he usually did, and he was convinced that he should enter the room. He pushed his way past the angry man, opened the door and walked in.

At first he could hardly see anything; the poorly lit room was thick with tobacco smoke. Gradually he could make out a collection of teenage boys and girls seated on benches around a table. As soon as he stepped in the room, two big fellows shut the door and stood in front of it. With any chance of escape cut off, Barnardo stepped toward the center of the room and began his sales pitch.

"I am here to sell you the Word of God," he said in the strongest voice he could muster. "You may purchase the entire Bible for threepence, or a New Testament for just a penny."

"Come on, old man, hand 'em over," one rough-looking boy said.

"None of your lip; let's have them books!" cried another.

But Barnardo was not to be intimidated. Leaping on the table in the center of the room, he called out, "Listen to me, all of you! These books cost me exactly twice what I am selling them for. If you really want them, you'll pay for them like honest men."

But the crowd, he realized too late, was roaring drunk and would not listen to reason. In an attempt to quiet them down, he offered to sing a hymn, but they drowned him out on the chorus. Finally, all his attempts to calm the group failed and the inevitable happened: they toppled him over, and he found himself underneath the upturned table with several of the larger boys jumping up and down on it. Then he lost consciousness.

Eventually he came to in his lodgings with two broken ribs and innumerable bruises. It took him six weeks to recover. A constable was summoned, who asked if Barnardo wished to press charges against the young ruffians. But Barnardo refused; he had invaded their premises at his own risk. To him it was a matter of turning the other cheek.

When the boys and girls were informed of Barnardo's decision, they were impressed—so much so that they gathered the next night and agreed that from then on they would make sure that the medical student was never injured again. Day after day during his convalescence, he was visited by some of the young people, inquiring after him. Their attentions almost became a nuisance, but Barnardo knew they meant well. And the incident had an effect that he never expected—an effect which paved the way for his future ministry.

"I believe this incident did more to open hundreds of doors in that particular quarter of East London," he later remarked, "and to give me a greater influence over the rough lads and girls of that quarter, than I could have attained had I been preaching or teaching among them for years."

As Barnardo continued his ragged-school teaching, it became clear that he could not conduct the Ernest Street School the way he knew best under the committee in charge of the institution. Therefore he resigned as superintendent and, along with a few friends, started his own school in the old donkey shed where he first met Jim Jarvis.

Until he met Jim, Barnardo was completely unaware (as were most people in London) of the existence of a tribe of "street urchins" who were completely destitute, without home or family. Either they were orphaned, or had been rejected by their parents, or had run away. How many were there? Barnardo had no idea, but Jim's bold claim that "there's heaps of 'em—more than I could count" was enough to convince the poor medical student that the problem was well beyond his ability to help. Yet the Lord was speaking to his heart, and he knew he had to answer the call—but how?

While he couldn't help all the homeless boys, he could help Jim. A few inquiries found Jim a place to stay—at least temporarily—in the home of a friend. He also was able to place a few other lads that came his way, but for the most part, his own resources were limited. Some months later in a Christian magazine called *The Revival*, he wrote an appeal for funds to help the children of Stepney. The response was modest.

Meanwhile, the young student had much to occupy his time. In the spring following his meeting with Jim, Barnardo joined a group of other Chris-

tians in distributing Bibles at an international expo-
sition in Paris. That fall he passed his preliminary
medical examination and registered as a student in
London Hospital, just in time to assist in a cholera
outbreak in East London. The cholera epidemic was
horrible; it gave Barnardo a more complete picture
of the poverty and filth of the East End. Throughout this time, he had a continuing sense of the Lord's
call on his life to do something for the people around
him, but he still didn't know what it was. The passing of his preliminary exams and his compassionate
service during the cholera outbreak had established
his medical reputation among the poor in the slums;
they were calling him Dr. Barnardo now, even though
technically he had some education to finish before
he could truly be considered a doctor.

Almost a year after his encounter with Jim,
Barnardo was invited to a missionary convention
being held in a large hall in the city. As a medical
missionary candidate to China, Barnardo was asked
to sit on the platform. The young man was a bit
uncomfortable being given a prominent seat in such
a large crowd, but he was just glad that he didn't
have to speak.

The man in charge of the convention, a Dr.
Davidson, stood up to announce that the main
speaker had been unable to attend at the last minute.

Then turning to the missionary candidate on the platform, he said, "Mr. Barnardo, why don't you come up and say a few words about your work with the ragged schools in the East End?"

Before he could get over the shock, Barnardo found himself standing at a pulpit before a crowd of perhaps several hundred. "I do not think I ever felt so unhappy in my life as at that moment!" Barnardo declared years later. He tried to turn down the invitation to speak, but Dr. Davidson would not hear of it. "Our main speaker cannot be here," Dr. Davidson said to the audience, "but we have here a young medical student, studying for service in China, who will tell us a little of his work with a ragged school in the East End of London."

Finding himself with no way out, Barnardo did what he always did when he was in a tight spot. He breathed a short prayer. Then he began to speak, haltingly at first, about his students and the teaching methods he had attempted to introduce. He was somewhat awkward at first, but gradually he warmed to the subject and soon was holding the crowd's interest. The topic of the East End of London led naturally to what had been on his heart and mind for months—the problem of homeless youngsters in that great city. First he described his initial encounter with Jim Jarvis, then other experiences he had as little Jim guided him night after night through the streets in search of children who were "sleeping out," as they called it.

While he described the poverty he found among these children, his emphasis always came back to their greater spiritual poverty. Who would lead these children to the Savior? Who would protect them from the thousand-and-one temptations that befell them on the streets of East London? By the time Barnardo wrapped up his talk with a heartfelt request for prayer for the homeless children of the slums, every eye was on him and every ear was tuned to his voice. He returned to his seat as the audience showed its appreciation for the message.

The meeting drew to a close and Barnardo stepped down from the platform; but before he could leave, a young servant girl approached him.

"Please, sir," she said, "may I speak with you?"

"Certainly," Barnardo replied.

"I came here to help the missionaries. I've been praying for them and thought I'd like to give something to help them. I'm only a servant girl, and I haven't been able to give much, but I did manage to set aside a few farthings for them.

"But sir," she continued, "now that I've heard what you've had to say, I see that not all the heathen are abroad. Some are at our very doorstep. I'd like to give what I've saved here to help your poor children."

Before Barnardo had a chance to respond, she placed in his hand a number of coins, wrapped in paper. "I felt not a little embarrassed," he said later of the incident. "It was the first public money I had ever received." What should he do? Should he take it or not? Up to this point, he and a few student friends had been providing the funds necessary for the school and for assistance to the destitute children. But this was the first time a stranger had offered him money, and he was awkward in his acceptance of it. When he got home later, the grand total was only a little more than six pence. But to Barnardo, the few coins wrapped in paper represented more than money. They were a sign to him of God's blessing on the work. He had been asking God for guidance; now he had his answer. "I have never doubted since then that this was God's way of showing me that He could by humble and unexpected instruments supply all that would be needed for any work which He gave me to do for Him."

Barnardo did not yet know it, but there was another result of his message at the missionary convention—his remarks were reported in the newspaper. He was soon to find out what an uproar a few simple words can cause.

4

∞

A Change of Direction

THE NEWSPAPER accounts of the young medical student's innocent remarks sparked a heated debate in the press. Several letters to the editor expressed shock that conditions such as Barnardo described could be allowed to exist. At the same time, other writers suggested that the stories of homeless children sleeping out in the open air were shocking because they were patently false. Perhaps, they argued, this medical student was exaggerating; perhaps he was the victim of an elaborate practical joke played on him by a group of slum children; perhaps he was an outright liar, hoping to profit by appealing to the sympathy of the public.

While this storm of controversy swirled across the pages of the daily papers, the young man at the center of the furor was blissfully ignorant of it all. What with his studies at the hospital, his work with the ragged school and his private reading of the Bible, Barnardo had no time to pick up a newspaper, and it was only much later that he discovered he had been living in the eye of a hurricane.

One man who did read the newspaper and followed the debate with great interest was the Earl of
Shaftesbury. The earl was a well-known champion
of the poor, especially poor children. His influence
had led to the passage of laws that kept children from
being forced to work long hours in factories and
mines. When he heard the story of children being
neglected in London and of the skeptics who doubted
the truth of this claim, he felt he could not rest until
he learned the truth.

Within a week after the missionary rally, young
Barnardo received an invitation to dinner from the
earl. The invitation said that the dinner would be
attended by a group of people who were very interested in the condition of homeless children in London. An opportunity to meet others who were interested in the same ministry was very appealing to
Barnardo, but he realized also how flattering it was
to be invited to dine with such a prominent man.
Before he accepted, he prayed that his motives might
be pure.

When Barnardo arrived that night, he found that
the dinner party included over a dozen guests.
Barnardo sat next to a prominent physician and
struck up a friendship that was to prove lifelong and
valuable; most of the dinner conversation, however,
consisted of small talk.

It was after dinner that the evening took a different turn. Lord Shaftesbury came up to young Barnardo as the guests were milling around in conversation and, with the ability of a man accustomed to taking charge of a situation, managed without a word to gain the attention of the entire room. The earl then began a friendly but detailed interrogation of the medical student.

"I have heard," his lordship began, "of your interest in the children of the streets, and I wanted to meet you and learn from your own lips whether the things I am hearing are true. I have heard it said, for instance, that you often find large groups of children asleep at night in various hiding places in different quarters of London without proper shelter or care. Is that really so?"

"Yes," Barnardo replied.

"Do you have any trouble getting these children to talk to you?"

"No, not once they see that I am truly interested in them."

"And are you ever able to get these children to leave their life on the street?"

"Oh, yes!" Barnardo was warming to his favorite subject. "I am often able to convince them to come with me at once, and have obtained help for them, but my ability to assist them has been limited by my finances." By this time, the group of dinner guests had gathered around the two men, listening to their discussion with great interest. "I suppose, then," Lord Shaftesbury continued, "that you would have no difficulty in finding a group of boys sleeping outside tonight?"

"Oh, certainly not," Barnardo replied. "Any time after 11:30 or so I could find, at one or two places I know of, quite a number of homeless children sleeping out all night."

Lord Shaftesbury looked searchingly at the young man. Barnardo didn't know this, but he was in the presence of some of his greatest doubters. The earl was inclined to have an open mind about Barnardo's story—he himself had seen some quite unbelievable examples of poverty and destitution in the city—but the men gathered in that room generally felt that the medical student was exaggerating or even making the whole thing up. There was only one way to come to the truth of the matter—the earl issued a challenge.

"Could you lead us tonight to one of these sleeping places?"

By this time Barnardo probably realized that his honor was at stake, but he rose to the challenge and said, "Yes, I will be glad to guide you to the children, as soon as it is late enough."

The matter was settled, and little more was said

until the hour of midnight. Cabs were called and the drivers directed to Billingsgate on the East End. Near the fish market in that neighborhood was a wharf where goods were loaded and unloaded from barges on the river; this was Barnardo's destination. A huge pile of goods was stacked there, covered with an enormous tarpaulin.

The other men saw nothing to indicate where homeless children might be sleeping, but Barnardo knew that they would hide themselves, for fear of being captured by the police. Followed by the puzzled group of dinner guests, the young medical student stepped up to the pile, found a space between two tarpaulins to insert his hand, and in a moment drew out a ragged, half-starved boy!

The child tumbled to the ground and, rubbing his eyes, began to cry and complain, thinking he had been caught. But Barnardo—and the others, who had by now recovered their voices—quickly reassured him they just wanted to help.

"Are you the only one in there?" Barnardo asked gently.

"No, sir," he replied. "There's a great many more chaps in there!"

"Well, do you think you could get them out if I gave you six pence for your trouble?"

"Six pence! Of course I will, sir! Just a minute

and I'll roof 'em."

Barnardo was puzzled. "What do you mean you'll 'roof' them?"

"Lemme show ya—the whole pile is covered with chaps, and this'll wake 'em up fine!" And before the men realized what he was doing, he hopped up on top of the pile and began stomping his feet. As soon as they learned he was stepping on the bodies of his fellow sleepers, they stopped his little dance—but not before it began to prove effective.

The tarpaulin seemed to come alive; its surface began to bulge and sink, like the waves of the sea. One boy after another appeared at the slit between the tarpaulins and, on seeing the group of strange men, tried to duck back inside. But the men were too fast for them and plucked each boy out as soon as he appeared.

Unfortunately, this still did not get them all out. The majority were still cowering inside, afraid to show themselves.

"Perhaps," the boy Barnardo was holding suggested slyly, "you could offer to give 'em somethin'."

Lord Shaftesbury spoke up with authority. "Boys, if you'll come out, we promise to give you each a penny* and something to eat." Suddenly the bottle was uncorked, and a veritable stampede issued forth

---

* About the price of an apple in those days.

from the gap between the tarpaulins. The fabric, before so tightly stretched, now began to sag in places for want of human bodies to hold it up.

When all the children had emerged, the men lined them up and began counting. There were 73 boys in all, most with no covering on head or feet. Lord Shaftesbury and his guests were speechless. Even Barnardo was amazed; he had been seeking out the hiding places of homeless children for almost a year and had never found more than a dozen or so at a time.

As he thought back on it in later years, Barnardo recognized God's hand in his finding so large a group of homeless boys. He was in the company of some of the largest philanthropists of London, men who were in a position to help him immensely. All he needed to do was convince them of the need—and that night in the East End he established the truth beyond any doubt.

The only question that remained now was where to find food for such a great hoard of children. Barnardo suggested a coffee shop he knew of in the neighborhood, "Dick Fisher's" by name, which was open all night. So off they went, a handful of gentlemen in evening dress and seventy-three ragged street urchins—a most unlikely crew. Dick Fisher was shocked by the sight of dozens of boys descending on his establishment in the middle of the night, but when he saw the distinguished gentlemen that accompanied them, he did his best to be hospitable. Soon each boy was warming his hands with a steaming mug of coffee and wolfing down slices of buttered bread. Lord Shaftesbury received change from the shop owner and placed the promised penny into every eager little hand. A cheer rose from the children that was deafening.

As they surveyed the scene in the coffee shop, the young medical student glanced over at Lord Shaftesbury and was surprised to see tears in the great man's eyes. "All London shall know of this," the earl whispered to him in a husky, determined voice. Later, as the group broke up to go their separate ways, the earl spoke warmly to Barnardo and urged him to continue his work with children.

This was only the first of several contacts with Lord Shaftesbury in which the subject of the East End orphans came up. Always a man who could recognize gifts and encourage their development, the earl counseled Barnardo to make the homeless children of London his life's calling.

Barnardo himself could see how his abilities and interest seemed to lie in that direction; he found himself eager to finish his studies each day in order to put in his hours seeking out and helping homeless children. Yet he was still undecided. His calling to China as a medical missionary had seemed so clear.

"Many of my advisers, among others Lord Shaftesbury himself, strongly urged me to give my whole life up to the waif children," he wrote later. "On the other hand, I still felt under the influence of what I believed to be nothing short of a divine call to devote myself to medical missions in China."

Beyond his calling was the practical matter of finances. Starting an orphanage would cost money, and where would it come from?

All these considerations he weighed over and over in his mind, and his prayers were filled with requests for God's guidance. He was so concerned that he not step out of God's will that he even prayed that God would stop him, by illness or death if necessary, from making the wrong choice. Finally the issue was settled as he read the Bible verse "I will guide thee with mine eye" (Psalm 32:8). From then on he determined to go in the direction that lay before him and trust that God would show him if he went wrong.

A month after the dinner party with Lord Shaftesbury he applied as a medical missions candidate to China Inland Mission, but was turned down for lack of training. This was the last of his hesitation. He never looked back after that. From then on he was convinced that he was called to stay in London.

Was the call to China just a false impression? Barnardo soon recognized God's hand even in that. "I now saw that the call to medical missions in China had been absolutely necessary," he wrote years later. "Without it, I would have never settled in East London, and probably never would have met my first homeless child." The "call" to China kept his commitment to the Savior alive, a commitment that had to be total and unswerving for the work that lay ahead of him.

For the rest of his life, he always considered the streets of East London his mission field. If he could not go across the sea, he could help others to do so. And it is interesting to note that even though he did not go on the foreign mission field, seventeen of his homeless boys did.

5

∞

"No Destitute Child Ever Refused Admission"

ENCOURAGED by Shaftesbury's support, Dr. Barnardo began to dream big. The children of the East End had to be educated, and boys like Jim Jarvis had to be given a place to stay. So it seemed logical that a ministry needed to be created that was not a ragged school or an orphanage, but included elements of both.

In 1868, readers of a major Christian magazine opened their latest issue to find an announcement of a new ministry being formed in the East End of London. A mission to the poor was being launched by Barnardo with an evangelistic "tea" meeting. (In England, "tea" is a mid-afternoon meal.) Readers were invited to contribute to the expenses of this new work.

When contributions were less than half what Barnardo hoped for, he scaled back his plan. But the first tea meeting attracted over 2,000 men, women and children—so many that they had to be fed in shifts. The long wait for food led to some rowdiness, but that stopped when Barnardo stood up to speak.

His preaching had an amazing effect on the restless crowd. They listened attentively; a number stayed for the altar call and were converted. In spite of this, Barnardo didn't consider the first meeting that successful. Perhaps he felt it appealed more to the stomach than the soul. At any rate, he began looking for a more effective way to draw an audience.

To publicize the evangelistic meetings, Barnardo and his helpers would march through the neighborhood before the service, carrying banners announcing its time and location. These little parades were often attacked by people throwing trash and spoiled fruit—at least at first. Gradually the workers began to win over the suspicious and cynical, and after a few months their campaign began to have an effect.

Ironically, their very success was their downfall. When a new owner took over the building where they held their meetings, he felt the tea meetings were hurting his tavern business down the street. One Sunday afternoon the workers arrived to set up for the meeting and found the doors shut in their faces. The owner had decided the hall was no longer available for rent.

Whether from frustration over this setback or the

frantic pace he had kept up for weeks, Barnardo became ill and was bedridden for two months. Without his leadership and no place to meet, the tea-meeting scheme collapsed.

Flat on his back and low on money, Barnardo soon discovered what good friends he really had. His small band of helpers refused to allow the ministry to die. Under his direction, they rented what Barnardo later described as "a small room in a poor street" and started a program of weeknight activities. One night the room was a ragged school; another night it served as a reading room; still another night they held a sewing class there. The results were so encouraging that the failure of the tea meetings was eventually seen as a blessing in disguise. The cost of renting the large hall had made it impossible to conduct as well-rounded a ministry as Barnardo's helpers could in a small rented room.

Like his thwarted call to China, Barnardo soon realized God's hand in the sudden end of the tea meetings. As his first major failure, it taught him a valuable lesson in dependence on God. Any confidence Barnardo had in his own abilities and plans was thoroughly surrendered to Christ. He also discovered that his previous work had not been in vain, for it opened the hearts of the residents of the area. He was now a familiar figure—and usually a welcome one—to the people of the East End.

In January of the next year Barnardo was well enough to personally begin searching for a larger meeting room. In March the ministry moved to two small cottages on Hope Place—one for boys, one for girls. And at this time the work was given its first official name: the East End Juvenile Mission.

Soon the mission had organized weekly prayer meetings and Bible classes for children, young people and adults. A wide variety of free services were offered to the poor—everything from a library to an employment agency. Regular church services were conducted each Sunday, with Barnardo preaching. The mission's Sunday school swelled to an attendance of over 300. Workers had to borrow benches from neighbors and set them out on the sidewalk to provide a place for the students.

In the meantime, Dr. Barnardo had not forgotten about Jim Jarvis and many other homeless boys in his ragged school, as well as those he met in his frequent nighttime explorations in the city. He had found temporary homes with Christian families for Jim and a few other boys. But there were too many needy children to solve the whole problem that way.

Besides, some of the boys had been on the street so long that they were too wild to be placed with a family. They needed discipline; they needed to learn the very basics of Christianity; they needed to be taught a trade, as well as how to read and write. Eventually these boys began finding a home at the East End Juvenile Mission.

The next year, 1869, the mission expanded to two more houses on Hope Place. The walls that separated the backyards of the four cottages were torn down and a roof put over the area, creating a hall to seat 300, yet the mission was still crowded. Every time they enlarged the space, they expanded the programs at the mission; every time they expanded the programs, more people came. By the spring of 1870, the neighbors were complaining about the crowds. Something had to be done, especially if Barnardo wanted to house homeless boys in addition to the Bible studies, ragged-school classes and various other activities at East End Juvenile Mission.

On a nearby street called Stepney Causeway, Barnardo found a large building that could be leased quite cheaply. This was to become the first of the Barnardo Homes. The only problem was it had to be renovated to make a suitable home for boys, and where was the money to come from?

Through word of mouth to the good doctor's friends and a modest appeal in a local Christian magazine, some contributions began to come in. The work on the building began; but because Barnardo refused to borrow money for the new venture, the renovations were often delayed for lack of funds. In a letter to a friend during one of the slack periods in contributions, Barnardo confessed, "I fear I shall be compelled in a few days to call off the workmen and suspend operations, as I am quite determined not to go into debt."

Finally, in December, the home was opened for business, and was almost immediately filled. By now it was four and a half years since Barnardo had set foot in London. The ministry seemed to be growing rapidly enough, but in the next few years it was to go through a virtual explosion. The cause of this amazing expansion was due to another of Barnardo's seemingly insignificant encounters.

It became a habit of Barnardo's to search the marketplaces and back alleys of East London for children sleeping outside. Late one night in May, he was a little too successful: though he had only five empty beds, he encountered over ten times as many homeless boys! Reluctantly he picked out five of the saddest-looking ones. It was difficult to choose, and he remembered the disappointment on the faces of several boys, including an eleven-year-old with flaming red hair named John Somers.

John, who was nicknamed "Carrots" by the other boys because of his hair, pleaded with the doctor to be let into the home. In the process, he told a little about his background.

Carrots never knew his father, and his mother sent him out on his own at the ripe old age of seven. He picked up a few odd jobs, but what he earned often wasn't enough to get him food and shelter. The only time he saw his mother was when she would catch him on the street, wrestle him to the ground, and take the few coins he had. Then she would disappear into the nearest liquor store for a bottle of gin. If he had no money, she would scream at him and beat him unmercifully.

Barnardo said about the experience later, "I had seldom seen a more unpleasant specimen of boy-life than Carrots." This was quite a statement from a man who had seen so many underfed and ill-treated children. All available beds had been taken, but the doctor gave Carrots a hot meal and promised that there would be room for him in about a week. The boy seemed satisfied with that and stepped out into the night with a hopeful heart.

A few days later, in an area of the city called Billingsgate, some workmen moved a barrel and discovered two boys, apparently asleep. The first woke immediately and ran away, but the other didn't stir. One of the workmen shook the boy, with no response. On picking him up, the men realized the limp, cold form was dead, the result of exposure to the cold and lack of food.

The boy was Carrots.

As soon as he heard, Barnardo came to where the body had been laid. Several homeless boys were already there, weeping over their friend.

"Did Carrots love Jesus?" the doctor asked one of the smallest of the mourners.

"Oh, sir, we never hears of Him," the child replied, "except when somebody's cursin' and swearin'."

"Well, you at least will hear something better," Barnardo replied, and took the boy into the home at Stepney.

The death of Carrots touched Barnardo deeply; he felt responsible. God had called him to rescue homeless children, yet he had turned this poor soul away from his door—all because he was worried about staying within his budget! Guilt can drive a man crazy or drive him to God. For Dr. Barnardo, it led to a momentous decision: he resolved before the Lord that he would never again turn away a child who was truly needy. As an act of faith, he hung a sign over the Stepney orphanage:

No Destitute Child
Ever Refused Admission

Some of Barnardo's previous supporters considered his decision impractical—even radical. Most other orphanages had stiff requirements for admission: the child had to be a member of a certain church, or had to have someone to vouch for him or make a donation.

Barnardo's orphanage changed all that. From now on, there would be only one requirement for admission: destitution. The child had to be without friends or family, with no place to live. Whenever a child showed up at his door, Barnardo would investigate the matter thoroughly. Often he was able to find a relative or friend who could provide a good home, but when no one else was available, he always took the child in.

"No Destitute Child Ever Refused Admission" became the rallying cry for an organization that quickly grew to gigantic proportions. The Stepney ministry soon expanded from one to five homes. Once Barnardo decided to completely trust God to provide for the ministry, he had his hands full—there were always plenty of homeless children.

But waiting for children to come to him was not enough for Barnardo. He began to seek them out himself. During the daytime Barnardo was busy with the ministry and his medical studies—yes, he was still working on his medical degree—and it was useless to look for needy children when they were up and about. They would run away before he had a chance to win their confidence. There was only one solution: he had to do his hunting at night.

6

∞

The Young Man
with the Lantern

IN HIS early years, while he was young and unmarried, Barnardo kept very odd hours. At the
time when most people were going to bed, he would
be lighting a lamp and putting on his hat and coat
to begin his nightly quest. In back alleys, under
bridges, behind sales booths in the marketplace—
anywhere a small child could hide—Barnardo would
wander about, shining his light. This earned him the
reputation in the neighborhood as "the young man
with the lantern."

Tramping through dark streets in the worst areas
of London was not the safest thing a man could do.
But Barnardo trusted that his Master's angels were
keeping watch, and he never suffered serious harm.
One night a gang attacked him, taking his hat, his
coat, his pocket watch and chain, his fountain pen
and all his money. As the thieves ran off, Barnardo
knew it would be a waste of time to chase them, so

he continued his search for children. A few moments later, one of the robbers met him and, to his surprise, returned everything. "We begs yer pardon, sir," the thief said with a smile. "Had we knowed ye was Dr. Barnardo, we would never've touched ye." Apparently the gang had found Barnardo's name on some of his belongings—and even in that rough neighborhood, his reputation commanded respect.

His reputation wasn't always an asset, however. Late one night Barnardo stepped into a "doss house"—a cheap, filthy boarding house where the lodgers often slept three or more to a bed. He was immediately recognized by a young girl who quickly called to her friends, "Here's the bloke who has taken away our pals!"

A while before, Barnardo had persuaded a group of boys to leave this doss house and enter a home for young men run by a friend of his. Little did he know that it would separate the boys from their girlfriends!

Suddenly the doctor found himself surrounded by a pack of angry teenage girls, who lost no time in taking out their revenge on him. They pulled his hair, slapped his face, tore his clothes and pushed him down. Once they had him on the floor, several of the girls held him down while others kicked and stepped on him. It took him some time to break away from the mob of wild females, but he finally got to his feet and ran outside.

Out in the safety of the street, he inspected the damage: his glasses were broken, his clothes were torn to shreds and he had bruises all over his body. Though it was probably one of the most humiliating experiences of his life, Barnardo took it in stride. In fact, he even wrote about the incident in the mission's magazine—and he included every embarrassing detail!

Another example of Barnardo's ability to laugh at himself was the story he told of *spending the night* in a doss house. After visiting so many of these filthy places, he was curious. What was it like to sleep overnight in one? He was determined to find out.

His guide in this adventure was Mick Farrel, a spunky little thirteen-year-old who claimed to have slept in most of the doss houses in East London. Mick said he knew of one place that had "swell chaps" as regulars, where for four pence (a very small amount of money) a person would be given a bed with "lily-white sheets" that was "fit for a king."

Barnardo knew that if he really wanted to experience the doss-house life, he had to look the part. So for a few days he went without shaving. After smearing his face and hands with dirt, he put on a battered felt hat, a red handkerchief, an old coat and some torn trousers. A piece of rope for a belt completed the disguise.

Soon Mick had led Barnardo down a narrow, foul-smelling street to a grimy building several stories high. Above the door was a sign reading, "Beds for single men, four pence." After some lighthearted conversation with the man who ran the place, the pair were directed to beds 17 and 18—"Where Gladstone [the British Prime Minister] always sleeps when he wants to be fashionable," the manager said with a laugh.

Their beds were in a room with over 30 others, mostly occupied by boys between ten and seventeen. The smell was unbelievable, and the "lily-white sheets" were a dirty yellow. None of this seemed to matter to Mick, who quickly undressed and hopped into bed, snuggling down with a contented sigh. "This is what I calls a proper doss," he declared, "and no mistake." Before he dropped off to sleep, he warned Barnardo to hide his clothes under his pillow, or they would get stolen.

What had begun as an adventure now seemed to be a foolish idea. Barnardo didn't know if he had the stomach to lie down in that filthy bed. Finally, his weariness overcame his disgust and he crawled between the grimy, yellowed sheets.

After nodding off for a while, Barnardo wrote later that he "awoke suddenly out of a horrible dream," in which he felt "pricking pins all over my body." Imagine his surprise to find that the painful sensations continued after he awoke! The gaslight was still on, so Barnardo could see that his hands and arms were covered with angry red sores.

"Alarmed, I sat up in bed," Barnardo continued in his retelling of the story. "The simple fact is that the sheet was almost brown with . . . moving insects which seemed to regard my body as their rightful property." The room was infested with bedbugs!

The insects continued to bite until Barnardo was in agony; he couldn't stand it any more. In desperation he shook Mick awake and cried, "Get up, get up at once! I must go out, or I shall go mad!"

"Why, 'taint nothin'!" Mick replied groggily, after Barnardo pointed out the army of hungry bugs. "I've seen 'em far worse—there were twice as many!"

Barnardo was in no mood to argue. After persuading Mick to get dressed, he rushed outside and took several deep breaths of fresh air. Then he hurried home and took a hot bath. When he looked in the mirror, he was shocked at his swollen, red face. "None of my friends would have recognized the face I saw reflected there," Barnardo wrote. "Three weeks elapsed before I was in a state to be visible."

It may seem hard to believe, but Barnardo often had to talk children into leaving the cold, hard life of the street and coming to his orphanage. Most of the homeless children he met had been mistreated by parents or other adults, and they didn't trust him. Besides, even though they were often hungry and cold, the street urchins enjoyed the freedom they had. It was the only life that most of them knew, and they couldn't imagine anything better.

But Barnardo could be very persuasive. And as word got around about how persuasive he was, some of the doss house owners began to see him as a threat to their business.

There was one doss house that Barnardo particularly wanted to visit, a very bad one in the Drury Lane district known as "Thieves' Kitchen." The name fit the place, because it was a notorious hideout and training ground for young criminals. Barnardo had tried for years to enter, but the manager, a big, rough-looking fellow, kept a close watch on the door. He knew who Barnardo was, and whenever the medical student paused at the entrance, he would growl, "Go about yer business!"

But one night, that all changed. Barnardo was walking past the Thieves' Kitchen, and the manager approached him with an anxious look on his face. One of the regular lodgers was sick with a fever, and the burly man was afraid that if it was contagious it could ruin his business. "Could you examine him,

Doctor?" he asked respectfully.

It was a chance to enter the forbidden lair, and Barnardo jumped at it. His patient, as well as most of the lodgers, was in his early teens, and the fever was nothing serious. Barnardo insisted, however, that the boy must remain in bed for two weeks—with frequent visits from his physician!

As Barnardo began coming daily to the boy's bedside, he kept his eyes and ears open and learned a few of the secrets of the Thieves' Kitchen. For one thing, the rumors were all too true: most of the boys were professional "lifters"—pickpockets. A brisk business was being done in stolen goods at the house.

Most of the boys could not read or write. One evening he brought a copy of *Uncle Tom's Cabin* to read aloud to his patient and discovered that he immediately had the attention of nearly everyone in the place. Once he realized this, he read the book at every visit, coming later at night when almost all the boys were present.

One night Barnardo noticed a tall, good-looking teenager and asked about him. "Why, that's Punch," one boy replied. "He's the king o' the lifters, he is! Lifts more than a dozen regular chaps—and he's never been caught!"

Barnardo wasn't sure what to think of that, but he noticed that Punch sat spellbound as he read the story. After several visits, Barnardo finished the first book and began reading *The Pilgrim's Progress*. Punch remained fascinated.

The two weeks passed and the patient was fully recovered. The boys were disappointed when they learned that the little man in the spectacles would no longer be coming by to read to them, but Barnardo had an answer. If they came to live at his home, they could learn to read for themselves.

Several boys wanted to be taken in at once, but Punch resisted, even though he obviously wanted to learn to read. Later, after he had learned more about the boy's past, Barnardo understood his reluctance.

Punch had never known his parents. He grew up in a government-run poorhouse, where he was very ill treated; at the age of nine he ran away. For a while he tried to earn a living selling matches on the street, but he got tired of sleeping out in the cold and being hungry all the time. Then one night in a doss house he met an older boy who taught him the "art" of the pickpocket. Before long he had surpassed his teacher and earned his reputation as the "king o' the lifters."

Barnardo was patient, but continued to gently press for a decision. Finally Punch agreed to live at the home, but only on one condition: if, after a year, he still could not read, he would be free to leave.

Though Barnardo did not normally allow a child

to set conditions on admission, in this case he agreed. However, Barnardo thought it best to keep a close eye on the boy, so he gave Punch little odd jobs to do, such as tidying up the office.

This gave Barnardo many opportunities to talk with the young thief and learn more about the boy's background. For the most part, he enjoyed his conversations with Punch, but it concerned him that the boy seemed to have no sense of right and wrong. To the "king o' the lifters," stealing was just a game—in fact, he was proud of it.

One day when Punch was bragging about his great "skill," Barnardo told him sternly to stop telling such tall tales. The boy didn't say anything but went back to work. About twenty minutes later, he asked the doctor what time it was. Barnardo reached for his pocket watch, but it was gone—along with the watch chain, his wallet, penknife and handkerchief! With a grin, Punch lifted a sheet of paper on a nearby desk to reveal the missing items.

Now Barnardo realized how serious the problem was. Preaching to Punch about stealing wasn't working; perhaps it was time to try a new approach. James, Punch's closest friend at the home, was known for his honesty. Dr. Barnardo pointed out that if James knew about Punch's stealing, it could destroy their friendship. A curious look came over the boy's face at this comment, but he didn't respond.

When Punch came into Barnardo's office a few days later, it was obvious he had been crying. With a sad look on his face he insisted that he be allowed to leave the home at once. When Barnardo asked why, the boy's sad face immediately turned to one of angry accusation: "You've been talkin' about me, haven't you?" he cried. "James has called me a thief."

In a gentle voice, Barnardo assured Punch that he hadn't said a word to James. At that, the dam of stubbornness broke in the boy's heart, and the doctor's office became an altar as the two knelt and prayed. From that day on Punch lost all pride in his thievery, and his past life was over.

By the time the one-year deadline was up, not only could Punch read but he asked to stay on so that he could learn the shoemaking trade. Within two years he was teaching other boys.

When Barnardo heard about an opening for an expert shoemaker to start a training program at another boy's home, he recommended Punch. Surprisingly, Punch was greatly upset by the offer. "You want to get rid of me?"

After Barnardo assured him that he would be missed, Punch began to see the advantages of the opportunity he was being given. He took the job and was an excellent example to the boys he taught.

This one-time thief became one of Barnardo's greatest success stories.

In the meantime, the East End Juvenile Mission, now popularly known as Dr. Barnardo's Homes, was growing at an amazing rate. The decision to admit any truly needy child, coupled with the doctor's nighttime habit of seeking them out, created a flood of children at the Mission's doors.

Barnardo and his staff managed the problem as best they could. Part of the secret to taking care of so many children was an efficient schedule. The day began at 6 a.m. with morning prayer. Between three square meals, there were two school periods, training in a trade or profession, physical exercises and sports, time for reading or meditation, and household chores—making beds, sweeping and scrubbing floors, washing clothes and other duties.

While "No destitute child ever refused admission" remained the rule of Dr. Barnardo's Homes, the staff was careful to make sure their boys were truly homeless. A background check was made of every child that was presented for admission to the Home. In some cases long-lost relatives or friends were found who were willing to take the child in. But for those who had no one at all who cared for them, Barnardo always found a place.

When he had no room in his orphanage, he often could find good Christian families to take in a child. Some of these families received help from the Mission to pay for the extra mouth to feed. Today there are many agencies that conduct this kind of "foster-parent" program, but in Barnardo's day it was a completely new idea.

To provide more room in his orphanage, Barnardo picked out some of the healthiest and most well-behaved of the older children to start a new life in Canada. Canada was still very sparsely populated in the late 1800s, and these older children were welcome additions to the growing country.

Despite these and other programs, the number of children Barnardo kept under his roof continued to grow.

But why were there so many needy children? Lord Shaftesbury was bothered by the question, and asked Barnardo in 1871 to review his records to discover the main causes of homelessness among the children in his care. What Barnardo learned from that bit of homework shocked him and was the beginning of a new field of ministry.

7

∞

The Capture of the Devil's Castle

BARNARDO'S review of his records brought to light a clear pattern: 85 percent of the children in his homes had no roof over their heads as a direct result of the drinking habits of their parents or other relatives. This was especially startling to him since he was not a supporter of the temperance (anti-alcohol) movement. He was even a modest drinker himself.

But when confronted with the facts, Barnardo willingly changed his convictions. He immediately pledged never to drink alcohol again. He also determined that a main thrust in his ministry to homeless children would have to be dealing with the problem at its source: the huge sales of liquor in the East End.

The poor people of London had almost no place they could go for entertainment and relaxation—other than the local "gin palace." One of the largest of these was the "Edinburgh Castle." Shaped like a medieval castle with a large, attractive and well-lighted entrance, the place did a thriving business.

Before the Israelites in the Old Testament went into battle, they sent a small group of soldiers in to "spy out the land." This seemed like a good idea to Barnardo, so he and some friends paid a visit to the "Castle." What they saw there shocked them. "Both bar and music hall were crowded, chiefly with young men and women," Barnardo wrote later. "A roaring drink trade was going on, and on the stage [immoral] songs were being sung. . . . Round the room were statues of the nude, which I suppose would be considered all the more artistic in that they were disgusting to decent people."

After praying for some time over the issue, Barnardo invited evangelists Joshua and Mary Poole to conduct a revival campaign in the city. The East End Juvenile Mission erected a huge tent within sight of the Edinburgh Castle and conducted revival services during the summer of 1872.

Under the inspired preaching of the Pooles, the response was amazing. Though the tent seated nearly 3,000 people, there were many nights that it was full to overflowing. Hundreds came to Christ that summer, and over 4,000 "took the pledge"—agreed to give up alcohol. Their names were recorded and they were regularly visited by their new-found friends, who gave them moral support.

Barnardo was astounded at the movement of the Holy Spirit during the tent meetings. "The scenes we are permitted to witness nightly are such as I never remember beholding during any previous period of my spiritual life," he wrote during the campaign. "Last Lord's Day evening 2,500 persons crowded to hear the Word of Life, and for hours afterwards we were occupied in dealing with anxious souls."

Many who were previously considered hopeless cases—drunkards, prostitutes and thieves—became lifelong volunteer workers at the Mission. And most of the new converts became members of the congregation that met every Sunday at the Mission. This group, referred to simply as "the Fellowship," was rapidly growing into a nondenominational church, with Dr. Barnardo as the senior pastor. The doctor preached each Sunday and tried to regularly visit all the members—all this in addition to his orphanage work!

The tent meetings were a rousing success, which created a serious problem: where were these new converts to be discipled? The Mission had expanded from two houses in Stepney to four, yet the congregation was still crowded—in spite of the fact that a fairly good-sized auditorium had been created by roofing over the backyards separating the four homes. Space had been a problem before the campaign, and now there were dozens of new people who needed a place to worship. "We have no place to bring them to," Barnardo complained in a report to a local Christian magazine. "The Mission Hall worked by our Mission for the last few years will scarce hold the converts."

But Barnardo's report also contained some good news. It seemed that the tent meetings had been so successful that some of the "gin palaces" were closing their doors—including the Edinburgh Castle, which was now up for sale!

Barnardo saw this as a great opportunity to make the "devil's castle" into the Lord's castle. Though it would need some renovations, the building had many aspects that would make it an excellent church and mission center, including a concert hall that could seat over 1,000. The only drawback was the purchase price—4,200 pounds. Although a reasonable amount, it was an unbelievable sum for a congregation made up of some of the poorest citizens of London.

Barnardo, however, sensed the plan was God's will and nothing would discourage him. He presented the idea to his friends, and soon donations began to come in. After much prayer the East End Juvenile

Mission signed a contract to purchase the Castle. The contract prevented the building from being put on the auction block—and with several others bidding for this prime piece of property, the Mission would almost certainly have lost out.

The Mission had fourteen days to come up with the total purchase price. At the time the contract was signed, less than two-thirds of the amount had come in, yet Barnardo was so sure of the Lord's leading that he was certain the money would arrive in time.

On the morning of the deadline, the Mission was still 110 pounds short of the total amount. At 11 o'clock a friend stopped by to make a final donation. It was a 100-pound note! Others stopped in to give, and by noon the entire amount was raised— with almost 100 pounds left over for renovations! The ink was barely dry on the deed when Barnardo was approached by the owners of a West End music hall, who offered to give him a 500-pound profit on his purchase!

A board of trustees was set up immediately. Six days later the first service was held in the transformed building. The People's Mission Church was formed, with Barnardo as pastor and a congregation of over 250. In only two weeks 55 others were accepted as members. Most of the Mission's other ministries were transferred to the Castle, allowing the Stepney property to concentrate on being an orphanage.

In the process of renovation, a question arose: What was to be done with the bar? As he stood in the middle of the central barroom and stared at the chandeliers, mirrors and brilliant colors, Barnardo admitted to himself that the decorations, though perhaps a bit gaudy, were quite beautiful. No wonder the average working man was attracted to a saloon! When a poor East End laborer slaves away all day in a dingy factory and comes home to an equally dingy little apartment at night, who could blame him for wanting to frequent a well-lit, happy and sociable place?

Then another thought occurred to him: Why not just leave the barroom intact? Of course, he would take down the nude statues and some of the other objectionable decorations, but much of the room could remain as it was. Scripture texts and inspiring pictures would be painted or hung on the walls. The entire building would be cleaned thoroughly. And instead of serving liquor, they would serve coffee and other nonalcoholic beverages. The "gin palace" would become a "coffee palace"!

In a flash he realized that this room would solve a major problem that he was already experiencing with his new converts: they had no place to go for wholesome relaxation and social contact. The only thing they knew in their past life was the barroom, but they couldn't go there and expect to avoid the temptation to drink. But here, in this newly decorated coffee palace, a man could come after a hard day's work and have a cup of coffee and some conversation with friends. He could take his family out to an inexpensive meal. He could read a magazine or newspaper, or join in a game of checkers.

When others criticized this seeming departure from a more "spiritual" ministry, Barnardo argued that he kept people away from the bad influences of the barroom by providing a healthy alternative. At any rate, the critics had little to complain about; the coffee-palace idea was so financially successful that it helped finance the other ministries at the Edinburgh Castle.

And the other ministries were extensive. Bible studies, youth meetings and other events were held in addition to an extensive ministry to the neighborhood poor. Much of the work was conducted full-time by a group of young women. These dedicated Christian sisters lived together in a nearby home called the Deaconess House. By living in the neighborhood and developing friendships with the residents of the East End, the deaconesses were able to learn who was in need and how they could help.

The ministry at the Castle was also the base for what became one of the largest groups of ragged schools in London. Every teacher in every school had come to the Lord through the evangelistic services at the church. The schools were known for their concern for the poorest of the students; for example, they regularly served meals to those children who came to class hungry.

After ten years the 1,000-seat sanctuary was becoming cramped, and the building, which was poorly built to begin with, was beginning to fall apart. The congregation banded together and rebuilt the church, creating a sanctuary that would seat over 3,000. In only a short time the membership increased and filled this sanctuary as well.

For thirteen years Barnardo served as the only pastor of the church, preaching two or three times on Sunday and visiting members during the week. As a preacher he was considered one of the best in London. "There were many wonderful conversions, and scenes of rejoicings, and songs of praise," recalled William Cuff, one of the earliest workers at the Castle. "Dr. Barnardo was the life and soul and movement of it all. . . . Such work was not at all understood then as it is now. Someone had to lead the way, bear the criticism, pay the price, and open the door. This Dr. Barnardo did with a splendid courage and a holy patience."

His pastoral ministry was an amazing accomplishment, considering that during these years he was still the full-time director of Dr. Barnardo's Homes. While serving as pastor of the People's Mission Church, Barnardo led his orphanages through their largest growth period.

By 1884, however, the workload became impossible, and Barnardo had to resign the pastorate. Many people in the church urged him to hand over the orphanage work to others and concentrate on pastoral work, but he refused. "I feel my Master has called me and given me as my lifework my children," he said, "and for nothing can I desert them."

It was just as well; the People's Mission Church continued to grow under other pastors. Though Barnardo still preached there frequently, it is to his credit as a leader that the church he started did not fall into decline after he left the pastorate.

The Edinburgh Castle was a major chapter in Dr. Barnardo's life, yet he began another important chapter at about the same time—marriage. Like so many other decisive events in his life, it became a gateway to new ministry opportunities.

8

∞

The Girls' Village

UNTIL 1871, there was no thought of romance in Barnardo's life—he was just too busy. Then he met Syrie Louise Elmslie.

Miss Elmslie was the daughter of a wealthy businessman in Richmond, southwest of London. She had grown up in luxury and was spoiled as only a rich man can spoil a child. She was educated by private tutors and her every desire was granted. Her religious education, however, was not considered important. Her family rarely attended church, and Sundays were usually spent in social activities.

At the age of eighteen, however, through the witness of the great philanthropist Lord Radstock and the evangelist F. B. Meyer, she gave her heart to the Lord and changed completely. Work with poor children in a ragged school in Richmond soon replaced her social activities. Like Dr. Barnardo, she was a great organizer and put all her energy into her work.

In the fall of 1871, Miss Elmslie organized a tea meeting for the poor children in Richmond. Having heard of Dr. Barnardo's success at similar activities, she invited him to come and speak. Barnardo was impressed with her ability to manage such a large event, and she admired the way his message kept the boys' attention. When they happened to meet the next day at the train station, Barnardo began to realize that his interest in her was more than just professional. And Miss Elmslie found herself strangely attracted to this gifted man.

Barnardo was so busy he had no time to follow up on his interest. It was eighteen months before they met again—also by accident—at a funeral. This time Barnardo took decisive steps, and within a few days they were engaged. Four weeks later, in June of 1873, they were married at a huge church in London, large enough to handle the crowd of well-wishers. This was followed by a six-week honeymoon— but Barnardo made sure he took some of his paperwork along on the trip!

Marriage opened new doors to Barnardo, doors that he had been longing to enter. Many of the boys in his orphanage had little sisters, and they begged Barnardo to take them in. In addition, Barnardo had seen some girls in his nighttime searches, but had been unable to help them. In Victorian London it would have been improper for an unmarried man to take in girls. Now that his wife was working beside him, Barnardo had the freedom to rescue homeless children of both sexes.

Friends who knew the couple's desire to start a home for girls went to work on a plan. By the time the Barnardos returned from their honeymoon, their desire was a reality. Mossford Lodge, an estate in the London suburb of Barkingside, had been donated, along with the funds to pay for renovations. The newlyweds moved in, and by October were ready to receive their first twelve girls.

Within a year the number had grown to fifty, but things were not going well. Some of the children's earlier lives had been appalling. One girl had tried to commit suicide twice. Another had "filled a baby's mouth with sand, and then sat on its face." These and other girls were housed in a barracks-style building and were made to conform to a rigid schedule. Needless to say, it was difficult to keep order.

But the true nature of the situation only came to light one evening as Barnardo overheard two of the girls talking. The conversation was filthy—and Barnardo realized with a shock that, "in what we thought was our happy little Christian home," the girls were being trained in sin! Because the girls were being housed in barracks, they didn't receive the supervision and adult influence they needed—and the older girls were teaching the younger ones the things they learned on the street.

Barnardo was completely disillusioned. "I was made to feel, as I listened with horror, that probably I had done harm, not good." With no other place to turn, he sought God in prayer. "I told our Father I was willing to give it all up at once and acknowledge . . . I had been wrong. With that, my peace of mind was restored."

He knew that God did not want him to quit, but he also knew the answer had not yet come. With the problem still weighing heavily on his mind, he went to bed and began to dream.

In the middle of the night, Barnardo sat up abruptly in bed and called to his wife, "Syrie, Syrie! It has been revealed to me how to deal with our girls." Then he quoted Psalm 68:6—"God setteth the solitary in families"—and checked his Bible to be sure he had quoted it correctly. Finally, he explained his dream to his bewildered wife.

In his dream, he explained, he saw a beautiful cottage with a light shining in its window. As he peeked in he saw a motherly-looking woman reading from the Bible, surrounded by several young girls. As he looked closer, he realized the girls were children from his home—but their faces had lost the hard, cold look he was so familiar with. Obviously the woman was having a wonderful influence on these girls. Then he overheard the Bible passage she was reading: "God setteth the solitary in families."

"Syrie, this is a revelation!" he exclaimed to his wife. "God means that our girls should live in family cottages with 'loving mothers' to supervise their homes!"

Immediately the next morning, Barnardo wrote to a Christian magazine that had often supported his fundraising efforts. With an excitement that came from a sense of God's leading, Barnardo outlined the plan for a "girls' village" consisting of dozens of cottages and a housemother for every fifteen or so girls.

However, days went by with no response to the appeal for donations. This was unusual, and it rocked Barnardo's faith in the new scheme. Was his dream just the result of an overactive imagination? Confused and uncertain, he decided to take some time off by attending some religious meetings being held in Oxford.

On the way to Oxford, Barnardo shared the train trip with a friend of his, a Christian brother he described as "a man of prayer, a man of faith, a man whose very face told you something of the peace of God which reigned within." Barnardo's face told a story as well, and his friend could see he was troubled.

"How is your work going on?" he asked, and Barnardo told him the story of the cottage idea and the lack of response from his usually dependable donors.

After a period of thought, Barnardo's friend asked, "If God shows you that your scheme is too large, are you prepared to give it up?"

A good question! Barnardo had never looked at it that way before. *I suppose*, he thought, *if God is not with me in this plan, it would be best if it didn't succeed!*

"Yes," he told his friend, "I am quite prepared."

"Then let us kneel down right here and commit your case to God," his friend replied. "Let us ask Him, if it be His will, to show you clearly, before you leave Oxford, whether you should go on with this idea or turn back."

The two men knelt down right there on the train and laid the problem before the Lord. On arriving at Oxford, Barnardo and his friend parted company but agreed to meet the next morning for breakfast.

Barnardo was getting dressed the next morning when there was a knock on his hotel room door. Thinking it was the bellboy with some hot water for washing, he said, "Come in."

A man stuck his head in the door. He was obviously just getting dressed himself, and his hair was still uncombed. "Is your name Barnardo?"

"Yes."

"You're the one thinking of building a village of cottages for little girls?"

"Yes, yes," Barnardo answered in surprise.

"Have you got any cottages yet?"

"No—not yet."

"Well, put me down for the first one. Have a good day." And with that the man was gone.

Throwing on the rest of his clothes, Barnardo rushed down the corridor, caught the man by the arm and persuaded him to come back to the hotel room and tell his story. It turned out that the man and his wife were mourning the loss of their daughter. When they read about the cottage idea, they decided to pay for one of the cottages in memory of their dead child. Later, he heard that Barnardo was staying in the same hotel, and decided on the spur of the moment to let the doctor know of their donation.

Barnardo spent some time praying with the donor and thanking God for the answer to his prayer. With a light heart, he went down to meet his friend for breakfast. Before he even had a chance to say anything, his friend looked at his face and quoted Isaiah 65:24: "It shall come to pass that before they call, I will answer; and while they are yet speaking, I will hear."

After that initial donation, other funds came in

to provide for several of the cottages. The "Girls' Village" was built in the community of Ilford, and the number of cottages grew with each passing year. The "cottage method" was such a success that eventually 40 percent of the children Barnardo rescued were girls.

Nowadays, the cottage method is a standard practice in homes for girls—and for boys as well. Those who run today's children's homes might be surprised at Barnardo's doubts about the success of his proposal.

9

∞

The Little Match Boy

THE DREAM that resulted in the Girls' Village is only one of many instances of supernatural guidance and help in the life of Dr. Barnardo. Throughout his ministry there were repeated evidences of God's hand on his work.

Like George Mueller, an earlier pioneer in ministry to homeless children, Barnardo could name many times that the Lord provided food or money as a direct answer to prayer. Mueller, however, decided that as an act of faith he should never ask for donations but simply present the need to God alone.

Barnardo admired and respected Mueller, and he didn't question Mueller's convictions, but he felt God was calling him to follow a different path. Barnardo brought every need to the Lord in prayer, yet he felt God wanted him to share the needs of his children's homes with his fellow Christians. He considered his ministry a privilege, and he felt it his responsibility to invite others to share in that privilege by giving. In fact, Barnardo often declared he had a "special mission to the stingy"!

And yet the most dramatic instances of giving were often unsought and unasked.

One winter, for example, was unusually cold, and the children were shivering in their beds at night. Barnardo's heart was breaking over the situation. He knew he must get extra blankets, but he had no money. So he did the only thing he knew to do—he took the matter before God in prayer.

After a painful night of watching his children suffer, Barnardo went to a wholesale supply house and picked out the blankets he wanted. The cost was almost 100 pounds, and since he had no money, he went away empty-handed.

The next morning, he received a letter from a pastor in another town, who had included a check "to pay the cost of additional warm clothing." The check was for 100 pounds.

Later in the growth of the homes, costs rose tremendously. At one point it cost 200 pounds per day just to feed the children! Unfortunately, though children have to eat every day, donors do not always remember to give as regularly. There were many periods when the donations received were just a fraction of what was needed.

During one such period, giving had fallen to a dangerously low level. Dr. Barnardo spent many hours in prayer over the problem, but it appeared that God was not answering. Day after day went by with no relief in sight.

One morning in May, as he sat in his office working, one of his assistants told him that he had a visitor. This was not unusual; he had many visitors every day. Most of the time one of the assistants could handle the problem. But in this case, the woman insisted on speaking with the doctor personally. After taking care of a few urgent issues, Barnardo brought the unassuming woman into his office.

Without even introducing herself, the woman said, "I have some money for you," and handed him a 1,000-pound bill.

Barnardo had almost never received a donation of that size. He had rarely even seen a bill that large. He stood there dumbfounded. But the woman was not done.

"I am familiar with your work, and I admire your cottages for girls." With that, she took a *second* 1,000-pound bill out of her purse and placed it in his hand. But still she was not finished.

"I am also pleased that you do not require your children in the cottages to wear uniforms," she added, and handed Barnardo a *third* 1,000-pound bill!

When he could catch his breath, Barnardo said he assumed the donor would like a receipt, and asked if she would like to give him her name.

"No, I would not," she replied, and before Barnardo could say anything else, she walked out the door, never to be seen again.

Barnardo almost thought it was a dream. But it could not be—there were the three bills still in his hand! When two friends stopped by, he shared the story and they joined him in praise to God for His provision.

But while God provided for Barnardo and his children, He often used Barnardo to provide for others. One of the most dramatic examples is the story of Billy Ryan.

One evening, Barnardo was hurrying home after a long board meeting when he was stopped by a small, high-pitched voice.

"Matches, sir?"

Looking down, Barnardo saw a small boy, running to keep up with him. Holding up two boxes of matches, the child called out, "Two boxes a ha'penny, sir. Buy 'em, sir!" Then, apparently thinking Barnardo didn't like the price, he added hesitantly, "Could give yer three boxes, but there ain't much profit!"

Barnardo stopped and took a good look at the little salesman. Writing about it later, Barnardo described him as "shoeless and stockingless, his bare feet well muddied, his trousers ragged, his jacket torn. Trousers and jacket were all he had to cover him from the drizzling rain and the shivering fog. A queer little old patched cap was perched on one side of his head."

The boy looked about eight years old, but Barnardo guessed he was probably older. Most children as poor as this boy were half-starved and short for their age. The doctor smiled down on the young street vendor and asked him his name.

"Billy, sir," the boy replied. "Billy Ryan."

"Well, Billy, have you sold much today?"

The boy shook his head sadly. "Only about six boxes, sir. That ain't much."

"Who sent you out?"

"Mother."

"And why does your mother send out a little chap like you to sell matches on the street?"

"Oh, she'd do it herself, sir, but she's awfully sick."

By asking a few more questions, Barnardo learned that Billy also had a sister—"She's littler than me, lots littler," he said—and they lived in a single room of a tumbledown house not far away. Since his mother was ill and his sister was too young to be out on the street, Billy had taken on the job of being the breadwinner for the family.

"Why don't you take me to see your mother?" Barnardo suggested. "I am a doctor, you know, and perhaps I can do her some good."

So off to his humble home Billy took this friendly stranger. He led his visitor up a creaky flight of stairs and ran into a back room. Barnardo waited politely outside the door. A few minutes later the door opened and a weak voice said, "Come in, sir."

There was not a stick of furniture in the room, yet the floor was very clean; the whole room, in fact, was neat and tidy. Obviously the family cared about their little home, humble as it was. The doctor described the place as having "a marvelous air of peace and even of comfort," despite the fact that there was no place to sit down. In a makeshift bed in the middle of the floor lay Billy's mother. Billy's sister, a bright-eyed little six-year-old named Bess, stood by her side.

When Barnardo said he was a doctor and asked how he might be able to help, the feeble woman told her story.

Mrs. Ryan was a widow, and had earned a modest living for herself and her children as a cleaning woman in the city. But one day she had injured her leg, and the wound would not heal. As the leg grew worse and worse, she soon became bedridden and unable to keep her job.

Barnardo listened to the brave woman's story with sympathy, then after checking her leg wound, suggested she go to the hospital.

"But what would become of the children?" she asked. "Billy might do all right for a while by himself—he is a brave lad! But little Bess . . ." and she broke down in tears. Barnardo was sorry he had made the suggestion.

"Well, then," Barnardo said gently, "why not try to get the children into some home or refuge, while you are taken to a hospital and properly treated?"

At this, the woman's eyes lit up. "Ah, yes, sir! That is what I would like to do, but I don't know how to go about it. But look here, sir." Then from under her pillow she took a leaflet and handed it to Barnardo.

"Read that, sir," she said eagerly. "I have been hoping and praying that God would let Billy and Bess get in *there*. I'd know they were safe and together, and then I'd go cheerful to the hospital!"

Barnardo looked down at the paper in his hand. It was one of his own leaflets. The woman had been praying to get her children into Dr. Barnardo's Homes!

With a humbling awareness that his visit was a direct answer to prayer, he replied, "My name is Barnardo. And if you are willing, I would be glad to take care of Billy and Bess until you get well."

In amazement, Mrs. Ryan called her children to her side. "Billy! Bess! This is the gentleman who has all the little boys and girls. I told you God would hear me, and now He's just sent him here to take and keep you both until I am well."

Stories such as Mrs. Ryan's were a great encouragement to Dr. Barnardo that God had placed His blessing on his work. That encouragement helped sustain him through one of the stormiest times in his life—a period in which Barnardo's enemies threatened to destroy his entire ministry.

10

∞

Struggles with Critics, Doubters and the Legal System

IT SEEMS it is almost impossible to accomplish anything important without creating enemies, and Barnardo created a lot. Barroom owners were out to get him for ruining their business. Workers in the homes whom he had fired for incompetence, laziness or dishonesty were angry with him. Parents who had turned their children out into the street were hoping to get their hands on them again, now that their offspring had been educated and taught a valuable trade. And of course there were always general gossips and busybodies, who couldn't or wouldn't believe that someone would work so hard for poor children without some secret and sinister motive.

The attack on Barnardo's ministry began with occasional rumors about the Homes, but nothing firm enough to be challenged. Then Mrs. Barnardo began receiving anonymous letters, accusing her husband of terrible sins and calling him a shameful hypocrite. Barnardo also received similar letters attacking his wife and other workers in the Homes.

At first, the workers at the Homes ignored the letters and rumors, but before long they grew more frequent and outrageous. The children, these gossips said, were half-starved and beaten, and were often punished by being thrown into rat-infested dungeons. The descriptions of these fictitious jail cells were wild: there were no beds; mud oozed through cracks in the floor; the victims were fed bread and water; and rats were even said to nibble at the boys' toes!

Anyone who was familiar with the ministry of Dr. Barnardo's Homes would have laughed at these rumors, but to those who were just hearing of the man and his work, the worst lies sounded all too possible. After all, how could all these stories have been started if there was not some portion of truth in them?

When the rumors were compiled and published anonymously by a social worker who claimed to be a fellow Christian, Barnardo made a grave mistake: he lost his temper. In the heat of anger, he gathered facts to refute the charges and handed them over to a friend. This friend published an anonymous letter in a local paper, defending Dr. Barnardo and discrediting his enemies. When Barnardo's critics responded with even greater attacks, the anonymous friend wrote a second letter, this time attacking the critics personally.

The lack of self-control and pettiness shown by the letter writer increased the heat of the argument. Soon the enemies of Barnardo were saying that the doctor himself had written the letters. They then accused him of blowing his own horn and trying to silence anyone who criticized him!

Barnardo was embarrassed by his friend's second letter. Though he appreciated the good intentions behind it, the letter was a poor witness for Christ. Even though it might mean losing a close friendship, he felt it was his duty to publicly reject the letter and state clearly that he had not written it. In a letter to *The East London Observer*, Barnardo described his friend's second letter as "atrocious" and "abominable," and commented with grim humor, "Well may I say, 'Save me from my friends!'" It might have been easier on him if he had revealed the identity of the letter writer, but he refused. The author's identity remains a secret to this day.

For two years the issue appeared to be closed. But the foes of Barnardo merely went underground. A new storm of controversy broke with the publishing of a 62-page booklet entitled *Dr. Barnardo's Homes, containing startling Revelations*. The booklet repeated the rumors that had been circulated earlier and even came up with more.

Barnardo's appeals for funds were clever lies, the booklet claimed. The photos of homeless children dressed in rags were faked. And the money he received for the poor he was spending on himself!

The old rumors of imprisoning children in dungeons, overworking and starving them, were all included in gruesome detail, as well as the charge that he had written the letters that caused so much controversy two years before. But worse than all these were new accusations:

• Barnardo had been seen in the company of drunken, immoral women.

• Barnardo had no visible income, so he must be dipping into the funds for the children to support himself.

• The children in his Homes were receiving no moral or religious training.

• Barnardo was not a physician, and had no right to call himself "Doctor."

The author of the booklet concluded that Barnardo was nothing more than a con artist, swindling his donors by appealing to their emotions with exaggerated stories of poor children starving on the street. The arrogant and hateful attitude of the booklet was evident in one of its summary statements:

"He who sees not these abuses is absolutely blind, and he who attempts to excuse them is absolutely insane."

The booklet was filled with half-truths and outright lies, but they were stated so cleverly that it was difficult to refute them. It was true, for example, that Barnardo had been seen in the company of drunken women; but his obvious purpose was to lead them to Christ. Jesus himself had the same accusation thrown at Him when He associated with sinners, and He responded, "It is not the healthy who need a doctor, but the sick. I have not come to call the righteous, but sinners to repentance" (Luke 5:31–32).

It was also true that Barnardo had no visible income. But he had no need to dip into the funds for the Homes because his father sent him a monthly living allowance to subsidize his work. He also received payment for various articles he wrote for magazines and newspapers. In addition, Mrs. Barnardo came from a wealthy family and had a large private income of her own.

The claim that there was no moral or religious training in the Homes was ridiculous. The children's daily schedule included morning and evening prayer, and the Bible was a regular part of the lessons in the ragged schools. Much more training in spiritual things was done informally by the staff. The criticism against the religious training in the Homes showed that the author had never investigated his charges.

The accusation that Barnardo had no right to call himself "Doctor" was one of the sneakiest of the booklet's statements. Though it was a minor point, the author of the booklet claimed it was evidence that Barnardo was an out-and-out fraud.

The whole argument hinged on the definition of the word "doctor." Strictly speaking, the only persons who could legitimately be called "doctor" were those who had an advanced medical degree, and Barnardo's schooling had been interrupted by his growing ministry. But in England it was common to give the title "doctor" to *anyone* who had at least some medical training. Barnardo had been called "doctor" ever since he began treating patients with cholera during his second year as a medical student.

Barnardo did not know how to respond to the booklet's attack. He could, of course, sue the author for libel, but Barnardo did not believe in taking someone to court. There was one action he could take— he could complete his medical training. Within a short time he was a licensed medical practitioner in London. Now, at least, they couldn't criticize him for being called "doctor."

Meanwhile, the rumors continued to swirl around

Barnardo's head, and his refusal to take the booklet's author to court made it appear that he had no defense for the charges. The Charity Organization Society, a group formed to keep an eye on charities, put Dr. Barnardo's Homes on its "cautionary" list, which put a cloud of suspicion over the ministry. If something wasn't done soon, public confidence in the Homes would collapse and the donations would cease.

Fortunately for Barnardo, he had some influential and creative friends who came up with a way to avoid a conventional lawsuit. They persuaded the author of the booklet to present his charges before a "board of arbitration." A senior judge, a prominent clergyman and a former Member of Parliament agreed to serve on the board. The government gave the board members full authority to issue a legal decision after they had heard the evidence.

For twenty days the booklet's author—through his attorneys—presented his case against Barnardo, calling forty-seven witnesses to prove his charges. Then Barnardo and his lawyer began their defense. They called sixty-five witnesses over eighteen days before Barnardo himself took the witness stand.

This was the opportunity Barnardo's accusers had been waiting for. By this point in the trial, they realized that their case against Barnardo was flimsy; they had failed to make any of their charges stick. Their only hope was to embarrass or anger Barnardo enough to get him to say something incriminating.

During cross-examination, the booklet author's attorney pressed Barnardo to identify his friend— the one who had written the two anonymous letters that caused so much trouble two years earlier. He obviously refused, saying that the author had repented of his rash statements and did not deserve to be made into a public spectacle.

Barnardo's accusers, of course, insisted that the letter writer's name was crucial information. When Barnardo continued to refuse, the booklet author and his lawyers gathered up their papers and left in a huff, hoping to create the impression that they had been treated unfairly.

The arbitration board was not impressed by the prosecution's dramatic exit—in fact, they saw it as a golden opportunity to bring the hearing to a conclusion. The members of the board had spent thirty-nine days hearing the testimony of over a hundred witnesses. During that time, all the charges had been thoroughly debated. The board had also made personal, on-site inspections of every one of Barnardo's orphanages. They had even ordered a complete audit of the ministry's financial records by a top-notch accounting firm. They were ready to pass judgment.

Five weeks later, the three board members issued a 10,000-word report, explaining their decision in detail. On the main accusation—misuse of funds—Barnardo was found entirely innocent. The accounting firm that checked the financial records found Barnardo's bookkeeping to be a model of efficiency. There was no evidence that any donations were spent by Barnardo for his personal use.

The board concluded that the children in Dr. Barnardo's Homes were well-fed and received a good education, including religious training. "We are of the opinion that these Homes for Destitute Boys and Girls," the board declared in its report, "are real and valuable charities and worthy of public confidence and support."

On some of the minor points, however, the board did find fault with a few of Barnardo's day-to-day practices:

• The rumors of rat-infested dungeons were the product of some gossip's wild imagination—but they had some basis in fact. Barnardo and his staff had occasionally put their most unruly boys in "solitary confinement"—not in a damp, dark cellar, but in a small room set aside for that purpose. The Homes had discontinued the practice by the time the board issued its report.

• The accusation that photos of homeless children dressed in rags were faked also had some basis in fact. The vast majority of photos that Barnardo published were of actual street children, but a small number had been posed. The board referred to the obviously posed photos as "artistic fiction"—concluding they were not intended to deceive donors, but were published merely to show what a typical homeless child looks like. Close-up shots of actual homeless children were probably hard to obtain— how could they get such a child to stand still long enough to take the picture? At any rate, the board decided there was no intent to trick the public.

• Though it was convinced that all the money donated to the Homes had been spent wisely, the board did not feel it looked good for Barnardo to serve as his own treasurer as well as the Mission's sole decision-maker. Reluctantly, Barnardo agreed. He had started his ministry as almost a one-man operation, but as the work had grown, he had failed to delegate the responsibilities. On the advice of the board of arbitration, the Mission formed a committee to help Barnardo oversee the work of the Homes.

The Apostle Paul promised that "all things work together for good to them that love God" (Romans 8:28). The storm of controversy that Barnardo went through was, in the long run, good for him and for his orphanages. It helped him identify and strengthen the weak spots in an otherwise strong ministry, preparing him for more fruitful service.

Later, his ministry went through other legal battles, mostly over the issue of custody of children. Barnardo would often take in children whose parents had abandoned them. Then, sometimes years later, the parents would demand the child's return, usually because their son or daughter had learned a trade and they saw they could make money through the child.

These lawsuits sickened Barnardo. He didn't want to see a boy or girl forced to live a life of poverty and starvation just so the parents could have money for liquor. One would think that the law would be on Barnardo's side, but it wasn't.

The law of England at that time gave parents absolute power over their children. Even if they beat and abused their children, parents had little to fear from the law. Even if they gave their children away to someone like Barnardo, parents could later demand them back. It didn't matter that they had signed an agreement to give Barnardo full and permanent custody—they could just change their minds! Under the law, a child custody agreement was just about worthless.

Barnardo lost these lawsuits, but the publicity they generated put public pressure on Parliament to change the law. The new law, which required parents to abide by a custody agreement, was popularly known as the "Barnardo Act."

None of Barnardo's later legal battles was as difficult as the first one—the hearing before the arbitration board. But they all had one thing in common: God used them to strengthen his ministry and publicize the needs of his children. All in all, Barnardo could look back at these struggles in the light of God's faithfulness—and even be thankful for his enemies.

11

❧

The Young Helpers' League

BESIDES helping Barnardo identify weak spots in his organization, the hearing before the arbitration board had another positive effect: it put Dr. Barnardo's Homes into the public eye. The board's conclusion that the Homes were "real and valuable charities and worthy of public confidence and support" was worth more than any amount of advertising. Donations increased dramatically; the public saw Dr. Barnardo as a man who had been unfairly treated by his enemies, and they gave to his Homes in record amounts.

The money was put to good use, because as Barnardo's fame increased, more and more children showed up at his door. By the time the board of arbitration issued its decision, Barnardo was completing his first eleven years of ministry and had rescued 2,000 children from the streets. In the next eleven years he would rescue over 12,000!

But one problem overshadowed the ministry during the years following the board of arbitration's decision: the donations were not keeping up with the increasing number of children. During his second eleven years of ministry, Barnardo rescued six times as many children, but he had to do it with only about four times as much money.

In spite of all that, Barnardo's vision never seemed to waver; he continued to dream big. His steps of faith were large ones, and often the committee formed to help him run the Homes had trouble keeping in step. In 1881, for example, Barnardo publicly announced his plan to start a "Youths' Labour House" to help the many young men who were unable to find work and lodging.

Lord Cairns, the committee president, was shocked when he heard about the plan. Without even informing his committee, the doctor planned to expand his ministry to include young adults! In a strongly worded letter, Lord Cairns threatened to resign if Barnardo insisted on going ahead with the plan.

But Barnardo was apparently as persuasive as he was full of faith. The Youths' Labour House opened later that year, and Lord Cairns continued to serve as committee president.

But as the years went by and the number of children continued to increase, Barnardo's slogan "No Destitute Child Ever Refused Admission" came into conflict with his conviction to "owe no man any-thing" (Romans 13:8). New buildings had to be built to house the increasing orphans, and some of the older buildings had to be renovated or replaced. After some soul-searching and much prayer, Barnardo decided that a mortgage on the buildings would not violate his convictions.

Some of his friends criticized him for this decision. There were times when he probably questioned it himself. For example, on one occasion he found himself facing a mortgage payment of 500 pounds during a time when donations were critically low. On the morning of the deadline for payment, he not only had no money, he even received another bill to pay!

Barnardo was on his way to the office of the lawyer who held the mortgage to ask for more time, when he was stopped by a British army officer. "I beg your pardon, sir," the officer said, "but aren't you Dr. Barnardo?" The officer explained that he had just returned from India. His commanding officer had asked him to deliver a donation to the Homes. The gift was enough to meet the mortgage payment—and the other bill as well!

The growing cost of the orphanages made necessary some streamlining. The Mission suspended some of the magazines it published and closed ministries that were not directly part of the work of the Homes. But the cost-cutting was not enough; there had to be an increase in giving. Some of Barnardo's friends suggested that he could increase the donations if he avoided mentioning religion in his appeals, but this he refused to do. There had to be another way.

On a cold November evening in 1891, after an unusually exhausting day, Barnardo sat down in front of the fire in his study. After brooding awhile over the wretchedly poor boys and girls he had admitted that day, he fell asleep and began to dream.

In his dream he found himself walking along the bank of a swiftly flowing river. Suddenly he heard a terrified cry for help. A boy was drowning in the river!

Barnardo began to run along the bank in order to get ahead of the boy, who was rapidly being carried along by the current. Finally, he threw himself down on the bank and stretched out to catch the boy—but he couldn't reach him!

Then Barnardo caught sight of some children playing nearby. He called to them to help, but didn't take the time to see if they heard him. He ran to another point and stretched himself out farther off the edge of the bank; the boy was coming nearer, but he still couldn't reach him.

Just as he was beginning to give up hope, he heard

a child's voice behind him: "We will hold you, sir; don't be afraid." The playing children had heard his cries and were holding his feet so he didn't slip into the river. Now he could reach farther! As the drowning boy came by, he was just able to grab him, and the other children pulled him back onto the bank. The boy was safe! With a cry of joy, Barnardo awoke from his dream.

In an instant, Barnardo realized the dream held the solution to his financial problem. "I could not save the poor helpless little waifs of the street by myself. I had not enough money; I had not enough strength; my arms were not long enough," he said when he described the dream to his contributors. "But the children, the happy children safe on the bank, were going to hold me and lend me their strength, and their courage, and their readiness, and we would unite our efforts for the great rescue work."

He had interpreted his dream to mean that the well-to-do children of England would help raise the funds needed to provide for his orphans. Within days Barnardo created a new youth organization for that very purpose: the Young Helpers' League.

Members of the organization received a magazine that told, from a child's perspective, the great problem of homeless children and how donations from the Young Helpers' League were helping to feed them and teach them a trade. Later, members of the League actually met the orphans they were helping in an annual event at Albert Hall, the largest meeting hall in London. The annual meeting included choral music, displays of over a dozen trades taught at the Homes, military demonstrations by the boys in the Watts Naval Training Home, and even some humorous skits—all put on by children. This way, the children that were members of the Young Helpers' League were able to see with their own eyes how their pennies and shillings had been put to good use.

Barnardo was hopeful that the Young Helpers' League might teach children the habit of generosity and bring in a modest income to the Homes. Perhaps, he thought, if the League caught on it might grow to a few thousand members. But the actual growth of the League went far beyond all expectations. Within ten years over 25,000 children had joined the organization, and by the time Barnardo died in 1905, the "pennies and shillings" given by its members totaled 144,000 pounds. Years after Barnardo died, the League continued to contribute over 50,000 pounds a year to the Homes.

The Young Helpers' League did just as its name suggests: it helped. But it didn't solve Dr. Barnardo's money problems. The worrisome issue of ever-increasing expenses and not enough contributions continued to weigh heavily on him, and may have even hastened his death.

12

"He Being Dead
Yet Speaketh"

AS the twentieth century dawned and Dr. Barnardo's Homes celebrated over 30 years of service, the strength of their founder began to falter. Barnardo's energy had always seemed boundless; it was common for him to work 18-hour days. So when his heart began to give him trouble, it was a shock to his friends and family.

His first attack occurred in May of 1895, after several days when he complained of feeling faint. The chest pains were so severe that he was afraid his next attack would be his last, so he wrote out his last will and testament. However, after a few weeks he felt almost fully recovered. "I do not doubt that, in answer to the believing prayers of many of God's children all over the world, I have been given back a large measure of my health," he wrote to one of the members of his staff.

The attack caused him to realize that he could

not continue the frantic pace he was used to. He usually arrived at his office early in the morning and left late at night. He often worked right through lunch and dinner, grabbing a sandwich or a snack instead of a full meal. Much of his time was spent in answering letters, interviewing job applicants, inspecting the living quarters of the children, and various other office duties. Most of the letter writing was to donors, and though there were hundreds, he personally answered many of their inquiries.

But the heart attack convinced him to change all that—or so it seemed. "I dare not work again as I did before I fell ill," he wrote to a helper. "To do so with my present knowledge of myself would be so far suicidal as to be sinful. For a while I must go very easy." His attitude sounded very careful and reasonable—until he explained what he meant by "going easy": "I must never be at my office later than six o'clock. Of course, once in a while I might go beyond this hour, but I mean as a rule."

But leaving his office at six did not always mean his workday was ended. He regularly took his mail home and answered it in the evening. With other reading he had to do, he was often up until well past midnight. Then he arrived at his office early the next day to begin the cycle all over again.

Why the heavy workload? Certainly he pushed

himself because of the great need, but just as strong was the fact that he truly enjoyed his work. "I would not exchange my life and work for any man's that I know of," he once said. "If I had to live over again, I would do exactly the same thing, only . . . with fewer mistakes."

His attempt to go at a slower pace was sincere, but it was hard for him to break his lifelong habit of energetic activity. As the needs of the ministry continued to demand his attention, he gradually went back to a hectic schedule. He had a few more bouts of chest pain, but for the most part he remained relatively healthy for a few more years.

During this time he opened several new homes and enlarged others. Among these were orphanages for children with handicaps and incurable illnesses, a naval training center for older boys, and homeless shelters called "Ever-Open Doors," which admitted needy children at any hour of the day or night.

He also took a trip to Canada to observe the branches of his work that had been started there. Canada was the key to one of Barnardo's greatest programs: emigration. Under this plan, boys and girls who had been taught a trade and demonstrated good character traits were matched with families in Canada. Much of North America was still frontier in the late 1800s, and the opportunities for work and success were much better than in London.

Barnardo was not the first to have an emigration program, but he became a leader in the method. During his lifetime he sent 17,000 children to Canada. The emigration program opened up a whole new life for these children, and provided more room in the orphanages for the ever-increasing flood of street children.

Another program which provided space in the orphanages was referred to as "boarding out." Barnardo looked for good Christian families with modest incomes—families that had love to give a homeless child though not enough money to support one. The mission would supplement the families' income so that they could take in an orphan. The idea was unusual at the time, but is now known as foster parenting—the most common way of providing care for homeless children today.

In the spring of 1901 he had a second heart attack and traveled twice to a special heart treatment center in Germany. By this time his lungs were also weakened, and his family insisted he travel to warmer climates during the winter months. He paid a third visit to Germany for treatment in the summer of 1902.

Barnardo was, by his own admission, a difficult patient. His trips to Germany could possibly have lengthened his life if he had been willing to set aside his work and allow the treatment time to succeed. But instead of resting, he had his mail sent to him and took a secretary with him so he could dictate letters. "He was always troubled at being away from his work," his secretary said of the days at the treatment center, "and would constantly think and speak of it."

As soon as the treatments in Germany began to have a positive effect and he began to feel better, he would return home to his work. "I am afraid if you were a doctor you would not like to have me as a patient," he confided to a friend. "I only obey my doctor when it pleases me to do so."

During 1903 Barnardo continued to have minor problems with his heart, but the main threat to his health came in the form of a train wreck. Three of his fellow passengers were killed, but Barnardo managed to escape the crash with several bruises and symptoms of shock. "Probably never in my life have I been brought as in an instant so face to face with death," he wrote later.

In early 1904, he suffered another serious heart attack and was ordered by his doctor to be treated again in Germany. The next year he became ill after attending the annual Young Helpers' League meeting at Albert Hall, and was sent again to Germany.

However, he suffered another attack during the trip; and after he arrived in Germany, he only became worse. Apparently realizing that this could be the end, he decided to return to England. His wife met him in Paris and nursed him for a few days until he was strong enough to complete the trip.

Barnardo arrived home on September 14th, and for two days was near death. Then, on the 17th, he felt well enough to look through his mail. The next day he called in his secretary and dictated some letters. On the 19th, he also dictated letters for several hours, then took a nap. When he awoke, he had a light meal, then called to his wife, "Oh, Syrie! My head feels so heavy!" After resting on her shoulder for a moment, he leaned back and passed away. He was 60 years old.

The news of Barnardo's death was a shock to the entire nation. Letters and telegrams of sympathy were sent to Mrs. Barnardo from all over, from rich and poor, from the slums of London to Buckingham Palace. But some of the most heartbreaking responses came from the children of England.

On the day after Barnardo's death a group of newsboys waited outside a London train station for the usual delivery of evening papers. When the carts containing the papers arrived, the boys began their usual rush to grab their papers, but suddenly stopped short.

The sideboards on the carts proclaimed the head-line: "Death of Dr. Barnardo." The crowd of boys was frozen in place as they read the sign. Not one moved to take his papers; they all stood in silent shock before the tragic news. An old friend of Barnardo's observed this little drama and stepped up to the crowd of boys.

"My lad," he said to the nearest of the young mourners, "the boys of London have lost a friend."

"Yes, sir," he replied, "and a good 'un, too."

Dr. Barnardo's coffin was taken to the People's Mission Church, where for several days thousands of people came to pay their last respects. The next Sunday a memorial service was held at the church. Though the sanctuary seated 3,000, hundreds of mourners had to be turned away.

The following Wednesday a funeral procession passed through the streets of East London. The crowd included 1,500 children from the various Homes throughout the British Isles. Thousands lined the streets to watch the sad procession, and businesses along the route closed up shop for the day.

The body of Dr. Barnardo was buried on the prop-erty of the Girls' Village Home, and a monument was placed there in his memory. But a greater monu-ment to his life was the ministry he left behind: by the time of his death, he and his workers had rescued 60,000 children from the streets.

At the gravesite, the Rev. Canon Fleming called for the nation to take over Barnardo's work and care for the poor children of England. And the people of the nation did, in a most practical way: they paid off the ministry's debts, which totaled 250,000 pounds. The cost of new construction and other special projects had put the Homes in a difficult financial situation, but the gifts donated in Barnardo's name allowed the ministry to be debt-free in a short time. The organization continues to this day as a helper to needy children all over the world.

Acknowledgments

THERE are many people who have helped make this book a reality. First and foremost, I want to thank my wife and family for the sacrifices they made to allow me the time to complete the manuscript. My younger son, Dan, helped tremendously by giving me feedback from a ten-year-old's perspective. The folks at East Shore Public Library in Harrisburg, Pennsylvania, deserve a standing ovation for tireless dedication in tracking down a number of obscure books and articles. Carol Wedeven showed me what a good friend she was by pestering me with postcards until I finished the project. Finally, I want to thank my prayer partner, Jim Doyle, for interceding on my behalf. This project was nothing less than a spiritual battle; he truly stood in the gap for me.

Several authors have preceded me in telling Barnardo's story, and because time and space prevented me from doing firsthand research, I owe them a great debt. The authors and their works include:

Barnardo, (Mrs.) Syrie Louise (Elmsie), and James Marchant. *Memoirs of the Late Dr. Barnardo*. London: Hodder and Stoughton, 1907.

Batt, J. H. *Dr. Barnardo: The Foster-Father of Nobody's Children*. London: S.W. Partridge and Co., 1904.

Bready, J. Wesley. *Doctor Barnardo: Physician, Pioneer, Prophet*. London: George Allen and Unwin, Ltd., 1930.

Neuman, A. R. *Dr. Barnardo As I Knew Him*. London: Constable and Company, Ltd.; Boston and New York: Houghton Mifflin Co., 1914.

Williams, A. E. *Barnardo of Stepney: The Father of Nobody's Children*. London: George Allen and Unwin, Ltd., 1943.

Wymer, Norman. *Dr. Barnardo*. London: Longmans, Green and Company, Ltd., 1962.

David E. Fessenden
February 1995

About the Author

David E. Fessenden is the managing editor for CLC Publications, the North American publishing house of CLC International, a literature mission working in over 50 countries around the world. With over 25 years experience in writing and editing, Dave has authored and edited many Christian books for adults and children. He and his wife, Jacque, have two adult sons.

This book was produced by CLC Publications. We hope it has been life-changing and has given you a fresh experience of God through the work of the Holy Spirit. CLC Publications is an outreach of CLC Ministries International, a global literature mission with work in over 50 countries. If you would like to know more about us or are interested in opportunities to serve with a faith mission, we invite you to contact us at:

CLC Ministries International
P.O. Box 1449
Fort Washington, PA 19034

—

Phone: (215) 542-1242
E-mail: clcmail@clcusa.org
Website: www.clcusa.org

DO YOU LOVE GOOD CHRISTIAN BOOKS?
Do you have a heart for worldwide missions?

You can receive a FREE subscription to:
Floodtide
(CLC's magazine on global literature missions)
Order by e-mail at:

floodtide@clcusa.org
or fill in the coupon below and mail to:
P.O. Box 1449
Fort Washington, PA 19034

FREE FLOODTIDE SUBSCRIPTION

| Name: _____ |
| Address: _____ |
| _____ |
| Phone: _____ E-mail: _____ |

READ THE REMARKABLE STORY OF
the founding of
CLC International

"Any who doubt that Elijah's God still
lives ought to read of the money supplied
when needed, the stores and houses provided, and the appearance of personnel
in answer to prayer."

—Moody Monthly

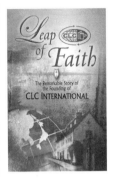

Is it possible that the printing press, the
editor's desk, the Christian bookstore, and
the mail order department, can glow with
the fast-moving drama of an "Acts of the
Apostles"?

Find out, as you are carried from two people in an upstairs
bookroom to a worldwide chain of Christian bookcenters
and publishing, multiplied by only a "shoestring" of
faith and committed, though unlikely, lives.

Read all the titles in the

FAITH'S ADVENTURERS SERIES

from CLC Publications

True stories of Christians throughout history who dared
to live by faith, and their adventures in following God:

- *Thomas J. Barnardo*
- *William Carey*
- *Fanny Crosby*
- *Mabel Francis*
- *Ann H. Judson*
- *Ira Sankey*
- *Hudson Taylor*

- *John Bunyan*
- *Nancy Chapel*
- *Ed and Doreen Dulka*
- *Grace Livingstone Hill*
- *Helen Roseveare*
- *Billy Sunday*
- *William Wilberforce*

Collect all 14 titles!

Ann H. Judson
of Burma
ISBN 0-87508-601-2

Colombian Jungle Escape
(Ed and Doreen Dulka)
ISBN 0-87508-092-8

Father to Nobody's Children
(*Thomas J. Barnardo*)
ISBN 0-87508-662-4

Freedom Fighter
(*William Wilberforce*)
ISBN 0-87508-659-4

Gracious Writer
for God
(*Grace Livingstone Hill*)
ISBN 0-87508-664-0

Ira Sankey:
First Gospel singer
(*Ira Sankey*)
ISBN 0-87508-471-0

God's Tinker
(*John Bunyan*)
ISBN 0-87508-462-1

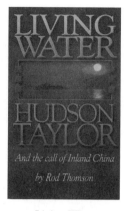

Living Water
(*Hudson Taylor*)
ISBN 0-87508-666-7

Only One Life
(*Mabel Francis*)
ISBN 0-87508-667-5

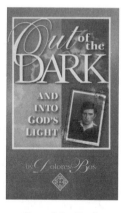

Out of the Dark
(*Nancy Chapel*)
ISBN 0-87508-720-5

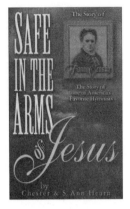

Safe in the Arms of Jesus
(*Fanny Crosby*)
ISBN 0-87508-665-9

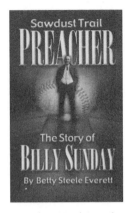

Sawdust Trail Preacher
(*Billy Sunday*)
ISBN 0-87508-499-0

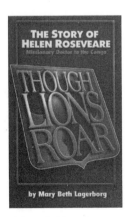

Though Lions Roar
(*Helen Roseveare*)
ISBN 0-87508-663-2

William Carey:
Missionary Pioneer
ISBN 0-87508-187-8